# Bubble,
# Bubble, Toil
and **Trouble**

# Bubble, Bubble, Toil and Trouble

MYSTICAL MUNCHIES, PROPHETIC POTIONS,
SEXY SERVINGS, AND OTHER WITCHY DISHES

## PATRICIA TELESCO

HarperSanFrancisco
*A Division of* HarperCollins*Publishers*

HarperCollins books may be purchased for educational, business, or sales promotional use. For information please write: Special Markets Department, HarperCollins Publishers, Inc., 10 East 53rd Street, New York, NY 10022.

HarperCollins Web site: http://www.harpercollins.com

HarperCollins®, 📖 ®, and HarperSanFrancisco™ are trademarks of HarperCollins Publishers, Inc.

FIRST EDITION

*Designed by Kris Tobiassen*

Library of Congress Cataloging-in-Publication Data

Telesco, Patricia.
  Bubble, bubble, toil & trouble : mystical munchies, prophetic potions, sexy servings, and other witchy dishes / Patricia Telesco.
    p.  cm.
  ISBN 0–06–259237–8 (pbk.)
    1. Cookery. 2. Food—Folklore. 3. Magic. 4. Neopaganism. I. Title: Bubble, bubble, toil, and trouble. II. Title.
TX714.T448 2002
641.5—dc21                                                                                              2002190216

02  03  04  05  06  ❖/QUE  10  9  8  7  6  5  4  3  2  1

**FOR THE KITCHEN WITCH IN EVERYONE!**

*This book is dedicated secondarily to Talyn,*
*who taught us to love cucumbers in a whole new way,*
*and to his "tossed salad" group of zany friends,*
*who are a family of a unique kind.*
*To them I say: Let-tuce celebrate!*
*If you feed them, they will come!*

# Contents

## 6. Knowledge Noshes and Education Rations

## 7. Employment Edibles

## 8. Fortune Foods

## 9. Happiness Helpings

## 10. Money Munchies

## 11. Pot of Promises

## 12. Psychic Platters

## 13. Relationship Refreshments

## 14. Safety Sustenance

## 15. Sexy Servings

## 16. Transformation Tonics

## 17. Vitality Victuals

# Introduction

Eat, drink, and make magick! These are very good words by which to live, and ones that this book happily advocates. Better still, *Bubble, Bubble, Toil and Trouble* shows you how to whip up a very special kind of magick *while* you're eating, drinking, and being merry: the kind that requires little more than thoughtfulness and old-fashioned ingenuity, but yields truly spectacular results. In fact, enchanted foods and beverages are perfect vehicles by which to feed spiritual hunger and quench mystical thirst, while titillating your taste buds at the same time.

Although you might normally conclude that there's nothing remotely magickal about breakfast, lunch, dinner, and their preparation, this book will change all that. Say farewell to ho-hum meals without any meaning, and say hello to spell-crafted magickal munchies.

See, *Bubble, Bubble, Toil and Trouble* is designed to help you think of your kitchen and the process of cooking in an innovative and delightful way. Consider the aroma of freshly baked cookies or the scent of warm bread, and how both tempt even the most stalwart of individuals into nibbling. When you do, is there a whimsical smile on your face? Do warm memories trickle into your mind? Does your stomach rumble just a bit? Yes! This reaction is exactly the kind of response that all the spell-recipes and processes in this book are designed to create when partnered with a little of your own spiritual vision and focus.

How? First, recognize that throughout history the kitchen has always been a special room, a kind of sacred space. And edibles and recipe components considered "soul food" can be found in nearly every historical and cultural setting. These foods are believed to manifest in specific personal or communal results when prepared properly and consumed. For example, in Japan people eat rice on their birthday for luck and wish fulfillment like we eat cake! In China eating apricots improves prophetic abilities, in Europe eating goose on Michaelmas Day brings prosperity, and in Scotland having pork on the spring equinox promotes longevity. Gives a whole new meaning to the modern phrase "You are what you eat," doesn't it?

Despite our fast-food society, there can be far more meaning to the entire cooking-and-eating process than simply feeding one's stomach. Now you'll be satisfying your spirit at the same time. Don't worry, this doesn't mean getting fancy. In fact, the entire philosophy of this book boils down to simplicity, pleasure, and fuss-free efforts. No "toil and trouble" whatsoever! You should never have to reach beyond your spice rack, vision, or personal abilities to make the spark of magick happen. Just open yourself up to the magickal potentials and possibilities that are around you every day, especially those in your own home.

I'm willing to bet that, if you think about it, you have traditions in your own household or from your family that have a bit of hearth magick in them already! What were your customary holiday dinners, and why? What do you eat when you're sick, and why? See, there are all kinds of foods and drinks that you already associate with specific feelings, circumstances, or effects! Now all you're going to do is put that association to good use, blending in a little positive energy to help the process along.

In Part I of this book, you'll discover the magickal potential in everyday culinary implements and how to activate that potential for a spiritual sauté, some simmering sorcery on the side, and marinated mysticism for full-bodied flavor! This section includes ways to turn any meal into a magickal masterpiece, even if it comes from a box!

Part II is the meaty portion of this book (vegetarians, forgive the word choice), filled with dozens of spell-recipes to enjoy or adapt to suit your needs. There's even some information on finding your own pantry protector, a god or goddess who can further bless and empower your creations! This section is set up by theme. So if you want to grill up some good luck, percolate passion, bake a little bounty, or simmer sensuality—tasty ideas and ambiance suggestions all await you here.

My cauldron's been busy cooking up this book—now it's your turn. Just turn the page, grab your wooden spoon, and start stirring up some magick today!

# PART I

# FROM CAULDRON TO TABLE

Food is magickal. To verify this, just watch anyone's face transform as they see their favorite meal appear from the stovetop or oven. Even the simplest of meals has the ability to fill a growling tummy and produce warm contentment! All you're going to do now is give the whole process a little more alchemical focus, saturating each ingredient with a healthy dose of whatever energies you most need.

Sound difficult? I promise it won't be. By the time you're done reading this section, you will have rediscovered the mystical and magickal potential in everyday culinary tools and ingredients, the hearth god/dess within yourself, and ways of honoring and manifesting the spiritual energy in each.

To begin, think about the way people used to treat the kitchen. Picture your grandmother puttering away, humming happily to herself over a secret recipe. Her joy filled every morsel of that meal. Likewise, picture a man telling his children a family story at the kitchen table. His focus on unity filled that room and any foods eaten in it. All this warm ambiance, and so much more, is part of the magick of the kitchen.

The art of cooking and the daily task of eating have also long been mini-rituals performed with family, friends, or even alone. To these mini-rituals each person added elements of personal taste, tradition, and culture for truly meaningful edibles filled with tasty, satisfying energy. The goal of *Bubble, Bubble, Toil and Trouble* is reclaiming this special spark in our homes every day. After all, we need to eat—so why not stir in a little spiritual sparkle to spice up the food?!

## WHAT STIRS THE CAULDRON?

So where does one begin? Exactly which tools, processes, and outlooks make for effective, meaningful kitchen magick? To sum up the ideology behind pantry enchantments: we should regard all things in this world as potential tools on the altar of our lives.

In kitchen magick, simpler items and methods work much better than complicated ones, because they allow the greater part of your focus to be on your intention. This makes the process more comfortable. In turn, any anxiety you may have about kitchen magick will disappear altogether when everything makes perfect, simple sense and when it feels really *right!*

KITCHEN MAGICK'S PHILOSOPHY

Everything you'll read in this book boils down to what could be called a metaphysical face lift—shifting and uplifting your spiritual outlook and demeanor to one that is playful and creative. Along with a fun-loving and inventive perspective, by far the best attitude to spoon liberally into your kitchen magick is one of self-awareness. There should never be discomfort or awkwardness in choosing, preparing, or serving spiritually augmented foods. Keep your inner voice active, and listen to it often when puttering in the magickal pantry. This voice will be your guide when you are trying to sort out personally significant ingredients and processes.

There need be no hocus-pocus about the energy you whip up in your pantry. What counts is your intention and the feeling you put into any process. In fact, at least 80 percent of the success in this area begins with common sense. You'll still be following the cooking procedures you're used to, and you'll still be using ingredients found around the house or at the supermarket.

The other 20 percent of the formula is summed up in five words: love, joy, intention, will, and wonderment. Love and joy have a magick all their own, and one that I'm sure I tasted in many of my mom's meals. She loved to cook certain dishes, and even when the meal didn't come out perfectly, the taste of her happiness filled every morsel.

Intention provides the whole process with a distinct focus, so the energy of love and joy can flow to the areas of your life where you most need them. Rather than just rambling through a recipe, you are

FROM CAULDRON TO TABLE

enacting each portion purposefully, keeping your particular goal in mind all the while. Magick is always a function of the will—of taking that extra step and truly believing that you can effect positive changes with but a thought.

In considering your thoughts, also consider your overall demeanor. Do not enter your kitchen with magickal goals in mind when you're angry, sick, tired, or tense. The negative vibes these conditions create may leech into your food and produce very real mystical indigestion. Under these conditions, I recommend treating yourself to take-out. Wait until a better time to whip up some magick.

Last, but not least, always trust your instincts. Around the kitchen cauldron there is no specific "right" or "wrong" way to perform hearth magick. Ultimately, the right way is the one that works for you. Keep this in mind as you read every spell-recipe that follows in Part II, so that the blend you ultimately create fulfills all your requirements in a personally pleasing way. Always stay true to your heart and vision, and you will rarely go wrong in magick—or in life.

## FROM STORE TO TABLE

Every ingredient in your spiritual sustenance has potential meaning for the whole, and the way the ingredients mix together will change both the food's flavor and its energy.

Think of it this way: when you bake a cake, certain ingredients must be present in the right proportion for the cake to rise properly and taste good. Magickal cooking works the same way, but has an added dimension—symbolism. Just as you normally measure and blend your cake's physical ingredients carefully, you also have to measure and blend the symbolic energies carefully to create a harmony of purpose.

Thankfully, kitchen magick offers you many different ways of doing this. The first way is the one we talked about already: your demeanor. Purposefully and sensitively putting together a meal or beverage is a huge part of what makes a successful magickal menu. Keep your mind on what you're doing and why you're doing it, and you're at least halfway to making magick already!

The second method is choosing a spell-recipe or ingredients for a spell-recipe that match your goal. Note: this doesn't mean that every single part of the blend *has* to have symbolic value. Managing that feat is possible, but time-consuming if you want the food to come out tasting right. Instead, try to concentrate on three symbolic ingredients (three is the number for body, mind, and spirit working together, which is the crux of kitchen magick).

For example, because "An apple a day keeps the doctor away," apple pie might be one good option for internalizing wellness. Cinnamon and ginger in the pie would support healing and victory (there, you've got three symbolic ingredients already). But what if you choose to make this pie to promote the health of a relationship? Substitute vanilla extract for cinnamon to manifest both love and passion. This flavoring doesn't hurt the pie in the least, and it has all the right vibrations necessary to help you achieve your goal. All that remains is to enjoy the pie, thereby internalizing the energy you've created.

At the beginning of each chapter I've provided a list of various spices, foods, and beverages along with their magickal correspondences to get you started, but this is really only a guideline. Trust your instincts. If an item has different meaning for you than the one I've given, make that meaning your magickal value. For example, if you associate apples with knowledge, then make an apple pie with walnuts and a hint of rosemary to improve your conscious mind! Again, all three of these ingredients support your goal, and you've made the process all the more meaningful by adapting it to your vision.

By the way, there are all kinds of extra ingredients (flavorings, nuts, toppings, tinctures, and the like) that you can use to round out the energy in your spell-recipes, as shown with the apple pie. Tinctures in particular are wonderful because they have such mild flavor that you won't even notice a change in the overall taste of the dish—and you don't have to use a lot! The amount of a particular ingredient has nothing to do with the power or symbolic value. Get away from thinking quantity; focus on quality.

A third means of kitchen magick considers the shape and color of your foods and beverages (and their components) for symbolic value. Every color has a distinct effect on the human psyche, which is a big part of what generates magick (your attitude again!).

Here's a brief list of color correspondences to get you started.

| COLOR | MAGICKAL APPLICATIONS |
|---|---|
| BLACK | REST, BANISHING |
| BLUE | PEACE, HAPPINESS, CONTENTMENT |
| BROWN | GROUNDING, FOUNDATION |
| GREEN | GROWTH, MATURITY, PROSPERITY |
| ORANGE | HEALTH, FRIENDSHIP, EMOTIONAL WARMTH |
| PINK | FRIENDSHIP, HEALTH |

| PURPLE | SPIRITUALITY, LEADERSHIP, CONFIDENCE |
|---|---|
| RED | VITALITY, ENERGY, PASSION, LOVE |
| YELLOW | COMMUNICATION, CREATIVITY, FERTILITY |
| WHITE | PURITY, PROTECTION, PSYCHISM |

So when you're feeling a little down in the dumps, try blueberries. When you need more financial security, consume a lot of green foods. Hey, even try a dish of green eggs and ham to release your inner child (mix your eggs with broccoli or food coloring for this effect). The key here is understanding the symbolism generated by the item's color and having confidence in that meaning.

Ah, but the idea of food coloring doesn't appeal to you? Okay, how about the shape of your food? The ancients often felt that if an item looked like something else, that shape was the god/dess's way of indicating its function. So, for example, they used heart-shaped items for love and phallus-shaped items for fertility. Here are four more that I came up with in looking at the shapes of some fruit at the supermarket this week. I'm willing to bet you can think of others without much difficulty:

1. **BANANA** EAT BANANAS TO ENCOURAGE MALE VIRILITY. AFTER ALL, HINDU LEGEND SAYS THAT THE BANANA WAS ORIGINALLY THE FORBIDDEN FRUIT!

2. **MELONS** EAT MELONS TO ACCENT LUNAR ENERGIES (ESPECIALLY MUSKMELON OR CANTALOUPE, DUE TO ITS PALE COLOR). TO QUOTE A MIDDLE EASTERN PROVERB, "HE WHO

FILLS HIS STOMACH WITH MELONS IS LIKE HE WHO FILLS IT
WITH LIGHT; THERE IS A BLESSING WITHIN IT."

3. **POMEGRANATE** FILLED WITH BRIGHT RED SEEDS, THE
POMEGRANATE SPEAKS OF ABUNDANCE, LIFE, AND THE
GODDESS (IT HAS A ROUND, WOMBLIKE EXTERIOR). TURKISH
BRIDES CARRIED POMEGRANATES FOR FERTILITY.

4. **STAR FRUIT** EAT STAR FRUIT AS PART OF MAKING A WISH,
JUST AS YOU MIGHT WISH ON A FALLING STAR.

The fourth way to support your spiritual focus is through ambiance.
The way an area looks affects the way you feel in it. Small sensual cues
(visuals, aromas, etc.) can generate much sympathetic energy for your
magick. Surround yourself with decorations, incense, candles, music,
or anything else that represents your goal and puts you in the right
frame of mind. I must confess that this particular helpmate makes for
some rather comical moments. Consider yourself standing in the
kitchen stirring an iron pot filled with thick, bubbly soup and chanting
over it. Shades of Shakespeare.

The fifth thing you can do to figuratively season your kitchen cauldron is to transform the process of cooking into a ritual. Cooking
already has strong ritualistic overtones. For example, you usually set
up your kitchen in a specific way for meals, cook certain recipes the
same way every time, and so forth. This repetition is a ritual. Now just
add the spiritual dimension.

How? Chant or incant over your food. There is a common invocative
bit of humor in the magickal community that goes "Rub-a-dub-dub,

thanks for the grub, yay goddess!" There's nothing that says chanting and incantations can't be fun. In fact, your playfulness and joyfulness are important—so long as a respectful, purposeful demeanor is maintained, I say go for it!

You could also visualize each part of your meal being filled with the bright, white light of Spirit. Or perhaps hold your hands over the top of the pot and think warm, loving thoughts. Use trial and error until you find a way to direct your desires into whatever you're creating. You can tell when you've done it right by the results! If, for example, you've made a bunch of happiness foods and everyone is laughing or smiling by the end of dinner, that's a success story.

Finally, although anytime is the right time for magick if your attitude is good, consider making certain foods during specific times to help the energy along. This is a very old custom. Even a hundred years ago people might bake bread or make beer when the moon was full so it would rise or ferment properly, for example. And since the kitchen is a place where we honor tradition, here are some ideas to get you started. Bake or brew:

**DURING THE NEW (DARK) MOON** WHEN YOU WISH TO BANISH NEGATIVITY, WEED OUT TROUBLEMAKERS, OR ENCOURAGE A RESTFUL NIGHT'S SLEEP.

**DURING THE WAXING MOON** WHEN YOU WISH TO INSPIRE SLOW, STEADY PROGRESS AND POSITIVE CHANGES.

**DURING THE FULL MOON** WHEN YOU WISH TO ENCOURAGE PROSPERITY, FERTILITY, INSIGHT, AND PSYCHISM.

**DURING THE WANING MOON** TO TURN AWAY ANGER OR DECREASE UNWANTED ATTENTION OR INTEREST.

**AT DAWN** TO MANIFEST HOPE AND ENSURE A POSITIVE BEGINNING FOR PROJECTS OR JOBS.

**AT NOON** TO STIMULATE THE CONSCIOUS MIND, LEADERSHIP ABILITIES, COURAGE, AND PHYSICAL STRENGTH.

**AT DUSK** FOR POSITIVE ENDINGS THAT GENERATE EMOTIONAL CLOSURE.

**AT MIDNIGHT** TO GENERATE MAGICK (IT IS, AFTER ALL, THE WITCHING HOUR).

Now, it won't always be possible to make a meal at the time specified for the results desired. But there's nothing that says you couldn't pre-prepare a dish at the "right" time when your schedule permits, then freeze, can, preserve, or refrigerate it until you need it. Get creative! Just remember to label these foods with their intended use before storing them safely away. Then when you open or defrost that item later, its associated energy is released to bless you just as surely as something made fresh! It's a great time-saver!

## DISHING IT OUT

We're not done yet! In thinking about creating a spiritual ambiance, don't forget food and beverage presentation. Even in those moments when you don't have consumables with the right symbolism handy for whatever your goal may be, you have other ways of bringing magickal symbolism to eating and drinking.

With beverages, think about the container in which you plan to serve them. A plain cup is perfect for magickal teas, but there's nothing that says you can't choose the imagery on the cup or its color to represent your goal. For example, serve a passion or love-potion wine in a pink wineglass.

Other good examples of symbolic serving ideas include:

**DRINKING FROM ONE CUP** FOR UNITY.

**PASSING ITEMS CLOCKWISE** TO INSPIRE BLESSINGS.

**DECORATING FOODS AND BEVERAGES** WITH UNIQUE TOOTHPICKS, UMBRELLAS, STIRRERS, AND THE LIKE WHOSE COLOR OR IMAGERY REPRESENTS YOUR GOAL; THE ITEM CAN THEN BE CARRIED LATER AS AN AMULET OR CHARM TO KEEP THAT ENERGY GOING.

**CHOOSING** A BOWL, PLATE, OR PLACE MAT FOR ITS COLOR OR IMAGERY.

**ADDING** AN AROMATHERAPY-INSPIRED CENTERPIECE.

**PUTTING** THE FOOD ON THE PLATE IN THE FORM OF A SYMBOL TO WHICH YOU CAN RELATE WHILE EATING, LIKE A SMILE FOR JOY.

**CUTTING FOOD** IN A SYMBOLIC IMAGE, LIKE A TOAST HOUSE THAT YOU CONSUME WHEN LOOKING FOR A NEW RESIDENCE.

In the kitchen cauldron's mix, consideration, cleverness, humor, and thoughtfulness are very powerful magickal tools too.

## PANTRY PROTECTORS

Many people around the world had and continue to have a god or goddess associated with and honored in the kitchen. People felt that the hearth housed special, loving energy that was often attributed to a divine form. The names and images vary, depending on the culture. Bannik, the Slavonic god of the household; Hastsehogan, the Navajo god of the home; Okitsu-Hiko, the Japanese kitchen god; Berchta, the Teutonic goddess of marriage; Fornax, the Roman goddess of ovens; Hestia, the Greek goddess of the hearth; and Mama Occlo, the Incan goddess of domesticity are just a few.

So what about your kitchen? How would you like to honor the Sacred there? Some keep a basic white candle in the kitchen that, when lit, represents the presence of the god/dess. Others like to pray or meditate before making magickal foods to invoke the Sacred. Still others like to lay out food as an offering, as, for example, in Santeria, in which someone honoring Obatala (a creator god) leaves a bit of unseasoned stew for him in a special place.

As with Obatala, many gods and goddesses had foods that were sacred and used as sacrifices. Do a little research on a divine figure that inspires the best in you, and then put out a small gift for this pantry patron or patroness on the stove with some incense or a candle. The key is taking a moment out of your hectic day and making room for the Sacred in whatever way you feel comfortable.

## THE DINING ROOM ALTAR

Once the food is served, whether for one person or many, please remember that the room has just become a sacred space all its own. Concentrate on enjoying what you've created rather than on any lingering tensions or arguments. In my home we hang a piece of mistletoe over the table to remind us of the "No Fighting at the Table" rule. Why? In Celtic tradition, when two warring armies met beneath a tree bearing this sacred plant, they had to put down their arms and not fight that day. See, it's not so much the mistletoe—it's the thoughtfulness behind it. It's just hanging there quietly, gently reminding us of the unity and harmony we value in our home.

Another simple way to keep the sacredness in the dining room is by reclaiming the tradition of mealtime prayers. According to a nineteenth-century bishop, prayer is "a wish turned godward." If you find that idea a little awkward, simply join hands with those at your table and tell each person there something positive. It can be something he or she did that day to make you happy, something you were thinking about, or perhaps even a quote you heard that you think would inspire everyone. The key here is connecting and staying connected—to each other, to Spirit, and to the warm, wonderful magick you've created in your kitchen.

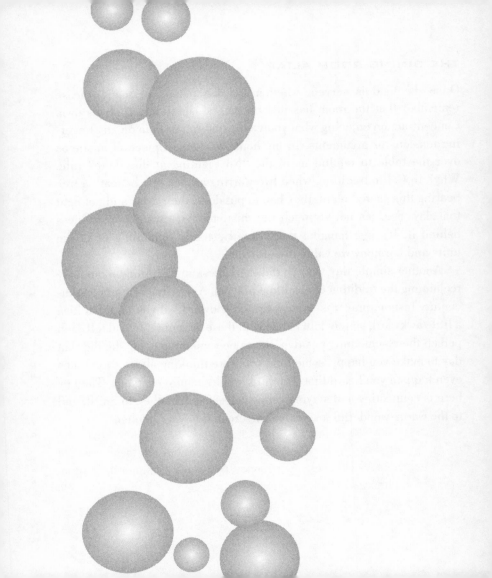

# PART II

# THE SPELL-RECIPES

## USING THIS SECTION

Part I of this book gave you the concepts and techniques necessary for successful, fulfilling, and fun pantry enchantments. Now it's time to get cooking! What kind of magick do you wish to whip up today?

This part of the book is organized according to your goals and needs. Think of a word or phrase that best describes the energy you desire; then look over the thematic chapters to determine which one best suits the situation. For example, if you need a little extra money, check out Chapter 10, "Money Munchies."

But what happens if you don't find a spell-recipe in that chapter that pleases your palate or your spiritual vision? Then it's time to get creative. Returning to the idea of cooking up money, try going to Chapter 8, "Fortune Foods," for a lucky windfall, to Chapter 7, "Employment Edibles," to get a raise or a better-paying job, or even Chapter 1, "Abundance and Fertility Fare," to help your money grow!

If all else fails, look at the ingredients listed for money at the beginning of the chapter and see if you can add or substitute a couple of them into a spell-recipe to give it the right meaning and flavor. Or, better still, make a special magickal recipe all your own! It's your kitchen, your sacred space, and there's no cooking guru here to please but yourself.

Vegetarians, fear not. Although your cauldron has some ingredient restrictions, they're important to your lifestyle. With this in mind, I've included many spell-recipes that suit your diet. For those recipes with meat as a main ingredient, by all means get creative in substituting nonmeat alternatives like tofu, tempeh, seitan, edible flower petals, and so forth. Just make sure whatever you substitute maintains the continuity of the spell-recipe's meaning in some manner. For example, tofu is a bean by-product, so it's an excellent ingredient for abundance- and money-related magick.

Meal magick begins in your mind and heart, not in preconceived notions of what makes for an exquisite culinary feast. Once you get past that point and keep your mind focused on your goal, your food becomes saturated with pleasure. After you eat it, this wonderful energy then manifests into your life literally from inside out.

# CHAPTER 1

# ABUNDANCE AND
# FERTILITY FARE

W hat do you want a little more of: joy, peace, truth, comfort, playfulness, savvy? No matter the goal, abundance foods will help you along. These spell-recipes create an internal richness and warmth that you carry with you everywhere. In turn, this will naturally bring more abundance your way, especially if you adapt the spell-recipe a bit so it better suits a personal need.

For example, if you're hoping to sow an abundant garden, use sunflower seeds as a nutty flavoring in a fresh salad. According to lore, sunflowers protect your garden and help it grow! Similarly, when you eat them, you can begin manifesting that "green thumb" you've always wanted. Or, what if you'd like an abundance of friends? To the same salad add some lemon, a fruit traditionally used in friendship spells.

Fertility is similar to abundance. The term is not, however, limited to physical fertility, but can apply to anything that you wish to flourish. For example, if you have a pet project that you really want to take off, fertility foods are a good starting point. Their energy can give your vision just the right nudge to make something truly spectacular happen.

For substitutions or additions to the spell-recipes below, traditional abundance and fertility components include:

Apples * Bananas * Barbecued foods * Basil * Beef *
Berries * Cabbage * Carrots * Coconut * Corn * Figs *
Fish * Grapes * Honey * Kiwis * Lettuce * Milk *
Mustard * Oats * Olives * Oranges * Peaches * Pork *
Rice * Tropical fruit * Walnuts

To add some special spiritual overtones, consider stirring your foods clockwise to attract positive energy, or cooking these dishes when the moon is full to inspire fullness throughout your life. Decorate your table with poppies and daffodils that have a quartz crystal in their vase to support the energies you're creating; these three items are metaphysically associated with plenty. For pantry protectors, call on Isis (Egypt), Ops (Greece), Agni (India), and Njord (Norway), all of whom inspire bounty and/or fecundity.

# Rich-Rewards Ribs

## (SERVES 3–4)

**P**repare these sticky ribs and watch all the money that comes into your hands stick to your fingers! In Celtic tradition those who enter paradise partake of pork in unending supply. Pork is also sacred to Keridwen, who represents abundance and fertility. To this symbolism we add honey for sweetness, ginger for power, and orange and mustard to round out the flavor on the grill.

**PREPARING YOUR CAULDRON** In the United States we often equate money with the color green, so put a green shirt on before you begin this spell-recipe (so you literally have a "green back"). Also surround your cooking space with rich things—gourmet coffee, a decadent chocolate, or anything else you associate with being really flush—to support the wealthy vibrations you're creating.

**COMPONENTS** * 2 sides baby back pork ribs * $1/2$ cup soy sauce * 1 cup orange juice * $1/3$ cup cider vinegar * $1/2$ cup apple juice * $1/4$ cup honey * 1 tsp. powdered ginger * 1 tsp. powdered mustard * $1/2$ cup minced chives or green onions * 2 Tbsp. minced garlic

**DIRECTIONS** Think about any obstacles standing between you and financial success. When you have those things clearly in mind, begin removing the membrane from the underside of the ribs (this helps remove those obstacles and make the meat more tender). Boil on low until the meat begins to retract from the bones.

Place the ribs in a large green- or gold-colored pan at room temperature. The color sustains the energy you're creating by surrounding the meat with the right hue. Meanwhile, in another pan, combine all the remaining ingredients and cook on low till the honey is evenly mixed in. Stir clockwise, saying:

*Honey make my fortunes sweet, Ginger make this spell complete.*
*Apple and orange for financial health, Come to me, good luck and wealth!*

Pour over the ribs and marinate them in the refrigerator for at least 3 hours so they absorb the spell. Brush the grill with cooking oil. As you do so, continue the energy you created with the marinade by adding an incantation like:

*Bless these ribs and the sacred flame,*
*Abundance grows and trouble wanes!*

When the grill reaches medium (about 320 degrees), grill the ribs for 75–90 minutes, turning every 15 minutes until the meat shrinks away from the ends (which also symbolizes financial troubles waning). Every other turn, baste with leftover marinade.

Serve as a main dish for three or four (hey, there's enough magick to go around, so share the wealth) during times of financial stress. Afterward begin making positive efforts that give the universe a chance to answer your spell. A windfall should come your way soon thereafter! Better still, this good fortune will not disappear as fast as it came, but will "stick" with you a long time.

**ENCHANTING ALTERNATIVES** Tinker with sauces and marinades.

# Bonus Beans and Rice

## (SERVES 6)

Ever try to play count the beans? There always seems to be so many, which is why they make perfect "plenty" foods!

The most famous Roman families were named after beans. Beans are associated with abundance, because of the number of beans that grow from one plant (there's the bonus!), and with providence, because beans were often a staple in times of need. There are over five hundred known varieties of beans, and they come in many shapes and colors—as diverse as you wish your blessings and bounty to be!

**PREPARING YOUR CAULDRON** To what part of your life do you want to apply this spell? Bring a representation of that into the kitchen while you're preparing this dish and try to pick your beans according to that focus. For example, if you want a prolific "green thumb," use green beans or peas to attract more "green" into your life. For physical "fertility," you might want to use yellow beans (the color of creative power) and bring a statue of a pregnant goddess into the kitchen.

**COMPONENTS** * 2 cups long grain rice, cooked * 1 cup sweet corn * 1 tsp. lemon juice * 2 minced green onions * 1 lb. precooked mixed beans (red, black, white, green, etc.) * 1 large tomato, chopped * 1/2 cup sliced olives (green or black) * 1 green pepper, sliced * 1 Tbsp. balsamic vinegar * 2 Tbsp. olive oil * salt and pepper, to taste

**Directions** After preparing the rice, leave it in its pan so it's as steamy and warm as is your spell! Add all the remaining ingredients and toss gently (you don't want to stir up any unwanted energy). For money, during the mixing process try the incantation:

> *Constraints shall wane, Within these beans, financial gain.*
> *Money to me, magick fly free, Today I claim prosperity!*

Repeat a money incantation four times. Four is an earth number associated with creating strong foundations. Serve Bonus Beans and Rice on a bed of lettuce, which looks quite pretty and adds to the symbolic value for the financial spell. Prepare this dish when you want your "hill of beans" to pile up faster than you can eat or spend them!

An incantation for garden abundance might be:

> *Green for sowing, energy's flowing*
> *From within to without. My garden's magick is growing!*

After you eat this dish, turn a teaspoon or two into the garden to transfer some of the good magick right into the soil.

If physical fertility is your goal, say:

> *Feed my womb with energy, Let life begin within.*
> *Born of love and bounty beans, The magick now begins!*

Consume the dish with your significant other while it's still steamy and then retire to a night of passionate lovemaking.

**Enchanting Alternatives** Any type of grain can be used instead of rice. The mixture can also be served cold with sweet peas as a garnish, to generate "cold hard cash."

# Frisky Figs

## (SERVES 2)

This makes a tasty side dish or dessert suited to inspiring a playful spirit and fruitfulness in any area of your life. Here the ancient fig, a fruit used in festivals honoring Bacchus to symbolize fertility, and "love" apples combine to make a sweet treat that will quickly manifest in literal or figurative fertility, with a little frisky foreplay thrown in for good measure.

**PREPARING YOUR CAULDRON** Approach this spell-recipe with a very frolicsome outlook, remembering that there's a lot of untapped magickal potential in joy and revelry. How do you "get in the mood" for this spell-recipe? Put on music that brings out your inner child, wear something liberating, and maybe even use an adapted children's rhyme to bless the sacred space of your kitchen, like this one adapted from "See a Penny, Pick It Up":

> *Cut a fig and cook it up, All this day I'll have good luck.*
> *Put figs with apples diced, Abundance and plenty, doubled twice!*

**COMPONENTS** * ½ cup dried figs, diced * 3 medium sweet apples, peeled and diced * ¼ cup sliced almonds or walnuts * 2 Tbsp. brown sugar * 1 Tbsp. butter * 1 Tbsp. flour * ⅛ tsp. cinnamon

**DIRECTIONS** Repeat your incantation eight times (the number of completion) while you preheat the oven to 350 degrees. Butter a small 3- or 4-cup ovenproof dish. Focus on your goal while you distribute the butter in the dish, then draw in the butter a symbol that represents the area of your life into which you want to bring abundance. For example, if you're hoping for a baby, draw a pacifier with your index finger in the buttery bottom.

Soak the figs for 15 minutes in boiling water. Besides making the figs tender, this cleanses them of any unwanted energies. Drain, and place the figs into a large mixing bowl with the apples and almonds.

While the figs are soaking, prepare the butter sauce, which will blend your magick into symmetry. Melt the butter slowly, and add the flour, sugar, and cinnamon. Cinnamon is a spice with real punch, so hold it in your hand for a moment and repeat your incantation again or say a prayer before putting it into the butter blend. Once the sauce is well integrated, pour it into the apple mix and toss till evenly coated. As you blend, use another verbal component that's repeated with every turn of the spoon like:

*Butter me up with bounty, Abundance come to pass.*
*Butter me up with bounty, By my will this spell is cast!*

Place the mixture in the baking dish and cook for 45–50 minutes until tender.

Serve warm to inspire "warm" feelings for physical fertility, or cold to motivate a cool head when it comes to wisely using your abundance when it comes.

**ENCHANTING ALTERNATIVES** Garnish the top of this dish with sweetened coconut or a drizzle of honey to further accent its energies and bring real "sweetness" into your life. If you want to specifically attract a plethora of friends, add $\frac{1}{4}$ tsp. of grated lemon rind to the blend. For fertile ideas, add two or three sprigs of rosemary.

# Horn-of-Plenty Pitas

## (SERVES 6)

A mong Mediterranean people, the olive was considered a precious gift, provided by the goddess Athena as a means of winning over Attica, which became Athens. The flavorful pita bread in this spell-recipe provides a warm, cornucopia-type womb in which to nurture your magick, and combines beneficially with the opulent olives nestled inside.

**PREPARING YOUR CAULDRON** Before enacting this spell, consider what kind of plenty you most need, and then choose the color or type of olives accordingly. For example, use green olives for financial abundance, black olives if you want abundant foundations on which to build and secure your dreams, or Greek olives to preserve your abundance once it arrives. Or, better still, blend all three together for a combined effect!

**COMPONENTS** * 1 lemon * 1 tsp. chopped garlic * 1 tsp. rosemary * 1 tsp. thyme * 2 whole bay leaves * pinch of salt and freshly ground pepper * $1/3$ cup fine-quality olive oil * 1 cup olives (your choice) * 1 lb. herbed feta cheese * 12 Greek pitas (6-inch size)

**DIRECTIONS** Slice the lemon into four wedges (four is the number representing sound groundwork), saying:

> *In the winds seeds are born. By the sun they are nurtured.*
> *By the waters, nourished. By the earth, given roots.*
> *So, too, give foundation to my magick.*

Place these slices with the garlic, rosemary, thyme, bay, salt, pepper, olives, and olive oil into a large container. Cover and refrigerate the mixture over the three days of a full moon (if possible; if not, a waxing moon will suffice). Each day at dawn (the time of hope), shake the olive mixture, saying:

*By the light of a new day,*
*I claim my plenty and give magick its way!*

On the third day (anytime), heat a ridged skillet on the stove on low. Brush each pita with a little of the olive oil mixture from the olives and warm it for 1 minute on each side. On each pita crumble some of the feta cheese and place a heaping tablespoonful of olives with a little of the liquid. Place the filling in the shape of a dollar sign to receive money, in the shape of a heart for love, and so forth. Finally, gently wrap the bread, which protects and nurtures your abundance, around the mixture and consume expectantly! You should see some significant change in your situation within three days or a multiple of three days (nine days, twelve days, etc.).

**ENCHANTING ALTERNATIVES** Add diced grilled marinated chicken to the olive and cheese mixture in the pitas. Magickally, this creates energy for an abundance of health.

# CHAPTER 2

# CLEANSING CUISINE

Someone once said that cleanliness is next to godliness (more than likely it was someone's grandmother!). Nonetheless, we're not going to take a bath in the soup pot anytime soon! Instead, the emphasis in this chapter is improving the spiritual cleanliness of the space in which we work our pantry enchantments, as well as designing dishes that purify our bodies, minds, and spirits.

Tackling the first part of this equation isn't difficult. Part of your "Preparing Your Cauldron" for every spell-recipe in this chapter is to take five minutes or so to straighten your work space. Clean the countertops with a little lemon or vinegar water, put out a white candle for purity, and generally make sure things look orderly. Try to create an atmosphere that feels and smells clean. This will support your spells on both the psychological and the sensual level.

When exactly should you go to the cauldron to whip up a cleansing spell-recipe? Anytime you literally feel dirty from the tensions or negativity of a long week or perhaps those generated by specific circumstances. With more people living and working in urban environments, where overcrowded conditions exist, it's much easier to accidentally pick up stray negative energy. For example, you're at the office talking to a disgruntled co-worker and afterward you notice your mood has changed. You feel weary or aggravated and have no idea why. Well, that co-worker just dumped his or her gloomy vibrations all over you! When things like this happen, the cleansing cauldron stands ready to be filled with the foods that will rout out the icky energy and replace it with renewal.

Traditional cleansing and purifying components include:

BARBECUED FOODS * BAY LEAVES * BEER * CHICKEN *
CINNAMON * COCONUT * FENNEL * GARLIC * GRAPEFRUIT *
HONEY * HORSERADISH * HOT PEPPERS * HOT SAUCE *
LEMONS * LIMES * MINT * MUSTARD * ONIONS *
ORANGES * PEPPERS (ALL KINDS) * RED FOODS *
ROSEMARY * SAGE * THYME * VINEGAR * WATER *
WHISKEY (OR ANY DISTILLED BEVERAGE) * WHITE FOODS

For the magickal dimension, prepare these foods during a waxing moon (so negativity shrinks) or stir counterclockwise. Decorate your table with finger bowls laced with lavender flowers and a pinch of salt. The flowers in particular are a nice touch as they support your magick visually and aromatically. Suitable pantry protectors known to have purifying powers include Kuan Yin (China), Kupalo (Slavic countries), Nerthus (Norway), and Faunus (Rome).

# Clean-Slate Garlic Chips

## (SERVES 4)

This marvelously simple spell-recipe cleans out your aura and skin pores so that you can literally start over with a clean slate in rebuilding your energy. Garlic is known both magickally and medicinally for its strong purgative energy. Mind you, follow this snack with a healthy dose of mints. In the immortal words of the Salerno Regimen, a text of health published in Italy during the Middle Ages, "Since garlic then hath powers to save from death, bear with it though it make unsavory breath, and scorn not garlic like to some that think, it only makes men wink, and drink, and stink!"

**PREPARING YOUR CAULDRON** Take a long, warm bath with a hint of lemon added to the water before creating this spell-recipe. Ritual baths are quite common among modern witches to help get rid of lingering tension that might hinder the flow of energy. Symbolically the bath also has a natural cleansing function, so you're basically doubling the effect of the spell here! Remember to visualize all the negativity and stress flowing out of your aura and into the water while you bathe and then going neatly down the drain!

**COMPONENTS** * 1 1-lb. bag hot chips (jalapeno, barbecue, etc.) * 1/4 cup butter * 4–5 cloves of garlic, finely diced

**DIRECTIONS** Preheat the oven to 300 degrees (heat has cleansing qualities too!). In a small pan on low, brown the garlic slightly in the butter. Using a pastry brush, brush the chips with this blend, saying:

> *Warmth without, cleansing within;*
> *By my words, this spell begins!*

Line a cookie sheet with several layers of paper towels. Place the chips on top and bake in the oven for 7 minutes (the number of completion). Eat while the chips are still slightly warm, so you can feel their energy moving into your body. As you do, visualize yourself being filled with sparkling white light that leaves no room for shadows in any part of your being!

**ENCHANTING ALTERNATIVES** Add some onion powder to the butter and garlic mixture for even more cleansing power, or serve the chips with a honey mustard dip. Honey accents physical cleansing, while mustard is an excellent overall purgative.

# Amuletic Onions

## (SERVES 6)

This spell-recipe helps you internalize the purifying power of onions and then bring that protective, clean energy into your surroundings. Egyptians considered the onion a symbol of the universe, while sailors ate onions to prevent scurvy. Magickally, onions were, and are, sometimes used as poppets (dolls) that absorb negativity.

**PREPARING YOUR CAULDRON** In keeping with the theme of this chapter, mop your kitchen floor or wipe the countertops with a tincture (1 cup water to 2 or 3 drops herbal oil) of sage or mint. This prepares the way for a "clean" flow of magick. You can also put onions on your windowsill in the kitchen or other parts of the house to act as natural negativity magnets. Remember to replace them regularly.

**COMPONENTS** * 1 10-oz. can chicken stock * 1 10-oz. can beef stock * $^1/_2$ Tbsp. brown sugar * 1 lb. red onions, peeled and sliced or chopped * $^1/_2$ lb. small Spanish onions * $^1/_2$ lb. small cooking onions * 1 bunch green onions * 2 Tbsp. cornstarch * salt and pepper, to taste

**DIRECTIONS** Preheat oven to 325 degrees, remembering that the hearth is the heart of your home and preheating can be a magickal prelude to your spellcraft if you approach it with a positive outlook. You can even consider blessing your stove by closing your eyes and placing your hands palm down on the surface while saying something like:

*What comes from my hearth, comes from the heart.*
*Here magick begins, with love from the start.*
*_____ [insert the name of a pantry protector], Bless my stove, your*
  *power impart.*

Mix all but $^1/_2$ cup of the chicken or beef stock with the brown sugar in a large ovenproof pot. Add the onions and cover, saying:

*Onions of cleansing, onions of power, I claim purity, hour by hour.*
*Through dish of onions, warm, Protect me ever from all harm.*

Bake in the oven for 2 hours. Meanwhile, mix the cornstarch with the remaining stock in a small pan till smooth. Cook on low till thickened, stirring counterclockwise (you want to banish any negativity or bad vibes). Remove the onions and stock from the oven and add the cornstarch mixture, blending well; add salt and pepper. This time stir clockwise and repeat your incantation again, perhaps three times for the body-mind-spirit connection.

**ENCHANTING ALTERNATIVES** Add some finely chopped red pepper (hot or sweet) to improve the cleansing power. Note that the leftovers from this side dish can be mashed and blended into gravy or soup for a rich onion flavor. The more concentrated the onion flavor gets, the stronger the purifying energy.

# Sacred-Space Garlic Chicken

## (SERVES 2)

T his is an excellent dish to consume the day before you undertake any special religious functions, bearing in mind that your body is a very real temple. The ingredients purify both mind and spirit, so you're in the best possible "space" for that undertaking.

In Christian tradition a white hen represents the purity of Christ. Hens were also regarded as suitable offerings for Athene and Demeter in Greece, Mercury in Rome, and Bride among the Celts. Garlic and "firewater" add to the symbolic cleansing value.

**PREPARING YOUR CAULDRON** Since you're making of yourself a sacred space, also take the time to work in a fully functional sacred space. Put a few of your magickal tools on the kitchen countertop, making it into a functional altar, and invoke the Quarters using a wooden spoon for a wand (point to the appropriate direction with your wand while invoking each element). A suitable invocation goes like this:

> *Powers of the east, come with the winds of transformation,*
> *Powers of the south, come with your magickal cooking fires,*
> *Powers of the west, come with the waters of cleansing,*
> *Powers of the north, come with the food for this spell.*
> *So be it!*

**COMPONENTS** * ¹/₂ head of garlic, peeled and separated * 2–3-lb. roasting chicken, cut into quarters * salt, pepper, and poultry seasoning, to taste * 1 Tbsp. olive oil * ¹/₄ cup bourbon or cognac * 2 cups chicken stock * 2 sprigs of fresh rosemary * ¹/₄ lemon * ¹/₄ cup light cream

**DIRECTIONS** Rinse the chicken thoroughly under cold water and pat dry, bearing in mind that you're also rinsing away any unwanted energy from the main component of this dish. Rub the chicken inside and out with a blend of the salt, pepper, and poultry seasoning, and insert whole cloves of garlic evenly under the skin, using a toothpick to secure them. This process literally massages magick into the meat and installs cleansing power (the garlic).

Brown the chicken pieces in a skillet in olive oil. Turn the pieces regularly, always flipping them counterclockwise so you're literally turning energy around. Once all sides are browned, move the chicken to a casserole dish, adding the liquor and chicken stock. Cook in a 300-degree oven for 15 minutes, uncovered.

Remove from the oven briefly and add the rosemary and the juice from the lemon while saying:

> *In this meal, the power of change, In this meal, the magick of love,*
> *In this meal, the freshness of cleansing, All blessed by the god/dess above!*

Cover the dish and then return it to the oven for about another 25 minutes until the chicken is cooked through. Remove from the oven and transfer the chicken to a separate platter. Place the cooking dish on low on the stove, slowly add the cream, and cook for about 8 minutes until thickened. Pour the sauce over the chicken, repeating your incantation one more time before serving.

As you and your guests eat, watch as the tensions and negativity flow away with every magickal bite. Serve with plenty of water to keep the cleansing power flowing.

**ENCHANTING ALTERNATIVES** Serve with a loaf of fresh French bread. Mash the baked garlic cloves onto the bread to manifest healthy foundations and pure motivations. Another alternative is to use crabmeat instead of chicken when you want to dispel a crabby disposition, using 1 lb. crab and all of the ingredients except for the poultry seasoning. Serve over rice.

# Cool-Head, Warm-Heart
# Horseradish Sauce

## (YIELDS 2–3 CUPS)

For cleaning out animosity, whether directed toward you or another person, this spell-recipe will do the trick. The horseradish purifies the negativity, while the frozen nature of the cream cools an overheated temper.

**PREPARING YOUR CAULDRON** Consider the source of your anger, and then choose an item over which to serve this sauce according to that focus. For example, serve this over poultry if the anger has to do with health or relationship problems, over beef especially when the problem is money or stability oriented, over apples when innocence has been lost, or over pork when you're upset over a lack of productivity.

**COMPONENTS** * 2 cups heavy cream * 1 tsp. sugar * 1 tsp. lemon vinegar * 4 Tbsp. fresh grated horseradish * salt and pepper, to taste

**DIRECTIONS** Whip the heavy cream to soft-peak stage. Slowly add the sugar and continue to beat until stiff. As you do, really release your anger into the beating process (if you have the patience, doing this by hand is great therapy!).

Hand-fold the lemon vinegar into the cream (make lemon vinegar by steeping ¼ lemon in 1 cup warm white vinegar for 1 hour, squeezing, straining, then storing for use). Finally, stir in the horseradish and salt and pepper to taste. Place in the freezer, saying:

*Quell my anger, my resentment wane,*
*Cleanse my spirit, bring peace again!*

Freeze the sauce until it reaches a frappé consistency. Spoon out over your chosen dish, remembering that applying the sauce acts like a salve on an open wound, soothing away the unwanted emotions and restoring balance.

Eat just before going into a difficult confrontation. It is always best to serve the sauce cold, so that you can keep a cool head no matter what happens.

**ENCHANTING ALTERNATIVES** Since this goes nicely with chicken, pork, and beef, consider making it into a sweet-hot sauce by adding crushed fruit (applesauce works), a dollop of maple syrup, or a teaspoon or two of brown sugar. Magickally, this sweetens a sour disposition!

# In-the-Pink Grapefruit Frappé

## (SERVES 3)

This tasty sorbet inspires overall well-being and physical cleansing specifically so you'll be literally "in the pink" for the rest of the day.

**PREPARING YOUR CAULDRON** In keeping with the overall theme of the spell-recipe, surround yourself with as many pink items as possible (like a pink tablecloth, napkin, plate, glass, toothpick, etc.). Pink has a very friendly, upbeat vibration that neatly chases away any gloom or icky feelings.

**COMPONENTS** * 5 cups ready-made pink grapefruit juice (*not* cocktail) * 1 1/4 cup sugar * 1/4 cup light corn syrup * 3/4 cup Spumante-style champagne

**DIRECTIONS** Place the juice, sugar, and corn syrup in a saucepan on low. Warm slowly until the sugar is completely dissolved, envisioning whatever problems have plagued you likewise disappearing.

Remove from the heat and stir in the Spumante. Pour the blend into a large pan and place in the freezer until it's slushy (note that freezing can also "freeze" negativity and sickness). Pour into a blender and whip until smooth.

Now, don a pink shirt, socks, or something else pink to symbolically put on "pink" energy. Consume the sorbet visualizing pink, bubbly light tickling your aura. You'll find yourself smiling and laughing soon thereafter!

**ENCHANTING ALTERNATIVES** Serve this over pink grapefruit, whose circular nature represents wholeness. For pure love, add a teaspoon of rose water to the initial blend, garnishing with a rose petal.

# CHAPTER 3

# COMELINESS CONCOCTIONS

There's an old saying: "Beauty is only skin deep." Not so with these wonderful spell-recipes aimed at manifesting attractiveness and confidence! On those days when you feel frumpy, puffy, homely, dragged out, or beaten up, comeliness foods will lift your spirits and put a confident sparkle back in your aura.

Some of the traditional components for beauty and confidence include:

APRICOTS * AVOCADOS * BASIL * BEETS * CUCUMBERS *
EGGS * HAM * HONEY * OATS * OLIVE OIL * PEANUT OIL *
PEARS * ROSE WATER * ROSEMARY * TEA * WATER

Beauty foods might best be prepared during a waxing moon (for improvements) or by candlelight (ever notice how everything looks nicer that way?). Also, comeliness meals should look as good as they taste to improve the symbolic value. Don't serve them in plastic dishes unless you want to look like Barbie or Ken!

Decorate your table with heather sprigs placed in a vase with an amber or cat's eye at the bottom to augment the energy you're creating. Some appropriate pantry protectors for this effort include Venus or Aphrodite (Greece, Rome), most certainly, Bast (Egypt), Apollo (Greece, Rome), and Balder (Norway).

BUBBLE, BUBBLE, TOIL & TROUBLE

42

# Here's-Lookin'-at-You Ham

## (SERVES 1)

For this spell-recipe we're depending on the saying "hamming it up" and the overall appearance of the dish to inspire self-confidence and a theatrical flair that concludes with a strong performance. Apricots encourage a sense of attractiveness; Brazilian lore says that pineapples were cultivated by Venus herself (a goddess who, I suspect, never had self-confidence issues)!

**PREPARING YOUR CAULDRON** You will want to look and feel your best for this spell-recipe. Put on something that makes you feel really special. As you don that item (or items), say:

*Puttin' on the ritz, puttin' on the glitz, Inside my heart, beauty sits.*
*Attractive without, beginning within, By my will, this spell begins!*

**COMPONENTS** * 1 large 1-inch-thick ham slice * 1 Tbsp. brown sugar * 1 tsp. cranberry juice * 1 tsp. orange juice * 2 whole pineapple slices * 2 apricot halves

**DIRECTIONS** Place your hands, palm down, over your ingredients before you start and repeat your incantation three more times. Three is the number of body, mind, and spirit in symmetry, something that also emphasizes the goal of beauty within and without! Afterward, mix the sugar and juices together and set aside.

Next, think of a simple symbol that represents beauty to you. A flower is one choice. Use a toothpick or knife to carve this symbol into the ham slice, keeping your goal strongly in mind. Grill on medium for about 30 minutes. Every 5 minutes, turn and baste with the blessed juice and sugar mix (think of this as applying makeup or other beautifying items).

Place the pineapple and apricot on during the last turn to warm in such a way that the pineapple becomes the outside of a pair of "eyes" and the apricot halves, the pupils. This way your ham will be *looking* at you, even as everyone else will soon be casting appreciative looks in your direction!

**ENCHANTING ALTERNATIVES** Energize the sauce with a little ginger, or adapt the spell-recipe for attractiveness to a lover by adding cherry, raspberry, or strawberry juice instead of, or in combination with, the orange (orange has energy for devotion too!).

# Alluring Avocado Dip

## (SERVES 3)

Avocados are used in cosmetics because they have natural moisturizing qualities. Magickally speaking, the rough outer skin hides the inner lusciousness, which is exactly what you want to bring out in yourself to charm everyone you meet that day.

**PREPARING YOUR CAULDRON** Eyes are the window of the soul, and since this spell-recipe relies on your eyes to communicate a message, it's important to treat them in a special manner. Lay a couple of cucumber slices or cool tea bags over them for about 15 minutes before creating this spell-recipe. This reduces puffiness and provides a fresh outlook for approaching your magick!

**COMPONENTS** * 1 3-oz. envelope lemon gelatin * 1/2 cup plain yogurt * 3 oz. ready-made avocado dip * 1/2 cup diced almonds

**DIRECTIONS** Prepare the gelatin as directed. Stir in the yogurt, avocado dip, and nuts, beating until frothy (this increases the ambient energy for your spell). As you do, recite an incantation like:

*Beauty within, confidence without,*
*Remove all fear, remove all doubts!*

Refrigerate 2 hours until firm (this symbolically "firms up" anything saggy, baggy, and frumpy, including attitudes).

Serve with sliced avocados as garnish, or perhaps a hard-boiled egg on the side (eggs are another beautifying food). As you eat, visualize yourself in the most positive way possible, then go out and meet the world head-on! You'll be amazed to discover how many people comment on noticing something "different" about you!

**ENCHANTING ALTERNATIVES** Substitute strawberry gelatin for self-love or orange gelatin for sex appeal.

# Come-Hither Cookies

## (YIELDS 3 DOZEN)

**O**ats are ruled by the planet Venus and are often used in facial masks to improve the skin's shine and tightness. Here, we're making them into a sweet treat to nibble when you're feeling a little self-conscious or frumpy. It will transform and fluff up your aura, giving you that irresistible "come hither" look.

**PREPARING YOUR CAULDRON** Put on an item whose color is assuring and uplifting to you. Red works very well as a power color, but whatever your choice, make sure it's vivid! You're trying to say "Notice me" and "Hey, I've got it together," and drab colors just don't portray those attitudes. Also, consider preparing this spell-recipe on Sunday, a day that supports the qualities of leadership, assurance, and poise.

**COMPONENTS** * ¹/₂ cup softened butter * ²/₃ cup packed brown sugar * 1 egg, beaten * ¹/₂ cup chunky peanut butter * 1 tsp. vanilla extract * 1 cup flour * ¹/₂ tsp. baking soda * ¹/₂ tsp. salt * 1 cup rolled oats * jelly (optional)

**DIRECTIONS** Cream the butter and sugar together to smooth the way for personal change. Add the egg and vanilla, beating well as you say:

*Charm, charisma, appeal; In this blend, my magick seal!*
*Allure, magnetism, and enchantment shine; And as I mix, I make them mine!*

Stir in the peanut butter by hand (peanut butter helps the magick "stick" to you) until smooth (again, you don't want the path to transformation to be bumpy!). Add the remaining dry ingredients. Mix well. Drop by rounded tea-spoonfuls onto a nonstick cookie sheet and make a dimple in the middle of each cookie if you are using jelly. Use strawberry jelly for self-confidence in a relationship, peach jelly for confidence in your wisdom, or orange jelly for confidence in managing finances. Fill and bake at 350 degrees for about 13 minutes.

Before you have to go out in public, eat one of these cookies, making a conscious effort to nibble away at any self-defeating attitudes you might be harboring.

**ENCHANTING ALTERNATIVES** Choose the flavor of jelly that focuses on your goals. If you want some attention at work, for example, mint is a good choice, since it represents prosperity and sweetens your breath! Apple improves your confidence for bringing peace to a touchy situation, and honey can be used to bring certainty with a health-related situation.

# Cute-cumber Salad

## (SERVES 4)

**B**eauty has many dimensions, and there is tremendous power in cuteness. When you'd like that rather innocent, adorable appeal, this salad serves the energy up just right.

Cucumbers have been cultivated for over three thousand years. They provide us with a cool head and have been used in cosmetics for a long time as skin softeners and/or whiteners.

**PREPARING YOUR CAULDRON** Don something white, the color of innocence. If the item is soft and cuddly, all the better (there's something about cuteness that makes people more huggable!). Bless the item, saying:

> _____ [type of clothing] of white, of spirit's light, give to me
> an aura bright!
> Filled with innocence and charm so fair, for as long as this _____ I
> wear!

**COMPONENTS** * 2 large English cucumbers (seedless) * 2 Tbsp. salt * 1/3 cup water * 5 Tbsp. red wine vinegar * 1 Tbsp. sugar * 2 Tbsp. minced dill weed * salt and pepper, to taste

**DIRECTIONS** Peel the cucumbers decoratively so that you have alternating strips of white and green. Magickally, this does two things. It provides a balance between earthy energy (green) and purity (white), so you're wholly approachable. Second, peeling the cucumber helps "peel away" unwanted self-images.

Slice the cucumbers very thinly. Place into a container and sprinkle with salt (a purifier). Chill for 2 hours. Drain any excess liquid created from the salting, which also drains away any unwanted energies. Place the cucumbers in a bowl with all the remaining ingredients, saying:

*Sugar for sweetness, dill for delight,*
*Pleasing all day, enchanting all night!*

Marinate in the refrigerator for 2 hours, shaking or stirring regularly so the cucumbers absorb the energy.

Serve with a sprig of dill for garnish and eat playfully with your fingers to help inspire the right attitude.

**ENCHANTING ALTERNATIVES** If you're hoping for physical appearances to inspire a bit of sexual attraction, toss 2 large stalks of celery, diced, into the blend during the marination. A couple of sliced tomatoes as garnish will increase the effect, but with more loving overtones.

# CHAPTER 4

# CREATIVITY'S COOKING

I n Celtic tradition, the goddess Keridwen owned a cauldron filled with the elixir of inspiration. Anyone who partook of this elixir was blessed with the muse. Such is my hope for your kitchen cauldron!

A witch's kitchen should always be a place filled with imagination and resourcefulness. Unfortunately, life doesn't always cooperate, and there are many days when being inventive is the last thing on our minds, let alone something for which we have any energy to spare! If this is the case, then these originality ingredients should put a fire back under any sources of inspiration that have grown cold:

ANYTHING MADE IN A POT OR SERVED IN A BOWL OR CUP *
ALLSPICE * CARROTS * CELERY * GRAPES * HAM * HONEY *
MEAD * MILK PRODUCTS * MUSHROOMS * MUSTARD *
POMEGRANATES * PORK * WATER * WINE

For continuity, present your creativity items in a truly inventive way. Make patterns on your plate that visually represent your goal and therefore support the energy you're creating. You'll want to stir these spell-recipes clockwise to attract a positive artistic flow, and possibly work during the full moon, which is said to increase our insightful nature. Another neat trick is opening a window that faces eastward while you cook. The east wind brings us fresh ideas and renewal.

For decoration, find a pretty egg-shaped stone to use as part of a centerpiece. Eggs are an ancient symbol of creation and fertile ideas. A suitable pantry protector for these dishes is, of course, Keridwen, already mentioned. Some others from which to choose include: Apollo (Greece, Rome), Indra and Sarasvati (India), and Ishtar (Mesopotamia).

# Muse Mead

## (SERVES 2)

**E**njoy a sip of this lighthearted mead whenever you need a quick boost of inventiveness, especially with your words. Mead is a honey wine that was very popular in Europe, especially among the Celts as part of nearly every social occasion. Honeyed wine also commonly appeared on altars as offerings in the ancient world, being considered a gift from the gods themselves.

**PREPARING YOUR CAULDRON** According to lore, you should pick grapes off the bunch from the top downward for taste, pleasure, and positive energy. This spell-recipe skips that step and starts with a prepared grape wine for people who have pressing schedules that don't allow for pressing grapes! However, if you have a bunch of grapes handy, it wouldn't hurt to honor this bit of lore in your spell-recipe by nibbling on them (from the top down) while you cook!

**COMPONENTS** * 1 liter white grape-based wine (dry) * 1 cup honey * 3 allspice berries

**DIRECTIONS** Warm the wine on very low with the three allspice berries (for the body-mind-spirit connection) to begin generating positive energy. Slowly add the honey, tasting regularly to make sure it's not becoming too sweet for you. By the way, if you can find heather honey, it's a delightful touch, as heather is a fortunate flower (I've often found that a little luck helps creativity a lot!).

Rebottle and chill, drinking a cup any time you need an inspiring nudge. As you quaff this beverage, release the magick you've placed in it by using an incantation as your toast. Here's one example:

*Grapes so pure, from off the vine, Let your creativity in me shine!*
*Honey sweet, with nectar blessed, Bring to me inventiveness!*

When sharing the wine, follow the Celtic tradition and pass the bottle to the right when pouring it out. This invokes blessings and unity.

**ENCHANTING ALTERNATIVES** Grape juice may be substituted for the wine. Or use apple wine or juice for wise and creative ways of handling relationships.

# Quick-Witted Potatoes

## (SERVES 4)

Looking for a way for your inventive nature to begin taking root and mani-festing in reality, especially in your words? The potatoes in this spell-recipe provide all the right foundations for just that, celery adds creativity, and carrots open your inner vision to capture something truly unique. And the spices will help you take those good ideas on the "road," so you're thinking on your feet while juggling other tasks.

**PREPARING YOUR CAULDRON** Blend 2 Tbsp. of cornstarch and 1 tsp. of powdered ginger. Bless this by saying:

> *Creativity and energy,*
> *Today and always walk with me!*

Sprinkle this in your shoes and put them on before you prepare the spell-recipe.

**COMPONENTS** * ½ lb. peeled potatoes, cooked and mashed * ½ lb. peeled carrots, cooked and mashed * ½ cup diced celery, sautéed * ½ tsp. celery salt * salt and pepper, to taste * ginger, to taste (optional) * pinch of sugar * 1–2 Tbsp. butter, melted * oil

**DIRECTIONS** Put all your components in a large bowl (a yellow bowl is best, as yellow is the traditional color of creativity). Stir clockwise, visualizing the area of your life where you most need resourcefulness. Oil a skillet lightly. Press the entire mixture into the skillet so as to make a large cake. Into the top of this potato cake etch a magickal image that represents an art, craft, or whatever else symbolizes your specific goal. The outer edge of the potato cake then becomes a sacred mandala within which your magickal energy will be warmed to perfection.

Brown over medium heat. Shake the pan every couple of minutes so the cake stays loose, cooking for 10 minutes in all. Flip the potato cake over carefully (do not break it—that would break your spell). Brown the other side for another 5 minutes.

Serve whole and cut just before eating, so that the desired energy is released just prior to consumption. Afterward, go back to the drawing board and see what wonders happen!

**ENCHANTING ALTERNATIVES** To be more creative in your relationship with another person, add 1–2 cups of grated cheese before browning the potato cake. To be more imaginative in your dealings with children, serve with sour cream, which accents maternal instincts.

# Lett-uce Invent Salad

## (SERVES 4)

**F**or those wishing to make a reasonable profit from their artistic abilities, this spell-recipe is ideal. It blends together the prosperous energies of lettuce, fertile peanuts, and zesty pepper with a wine vinaigrette for guaranteed success!

**PREPARING YOUR CAULDRON** Into a 3 x 3-inch square of yellow and green fabric (yellow represents the creative self, while green symbolizes money-making) place four peanuts (the number of earth and financial foundations), a pinch of mustard and pepper, and a little parsley—all of which you have for your spell-recipe. Bless this, saying:

*From my vision, from my heart, From my work, wondrous art.*
*From my vision, from my heart, Fortune flows, prosperity impart!*

**COMPONENTS** * 4 cups mixed romaine, radicchio, Bibb lettuce, and curly endive * ¹/₄ cup peanuts * ¹/₂ cup olive oil * ¹/₂ cup red wine vinegar * ¹/₂ tsp. dry mustard * ¹/₄ tsp. cayenne (or to taste) * 1 Tbsp. parsley, finely chopped * salt and pepper, to taste

**DIRECTIONS** Rinse the lettuce to remove any unwanted energy and gently tear it (according to folklore, you should never cut lettuce, as it will cut off your prosperity). Place in a large yellow or green bowl so the color of the container surrounds the lettuce with supportive energy. In another container mix the oil, vinegar, and spices. Shake well to "shake up" the energy. Chill, and shake vigorously again before pouring over the lettuce.

Serve as a side dish suited to any ingenious feast. Once you're done eating, get on the Internet and write up an ad for your work, apply for a grant, or design a proposal and send it off. Money should follow soon.

**ENCHANTING ALTERNATIVES** Substitute rosemary, basil, and oregano for the mustard and cayenne to create a good memory for working with your art or craft or a strong devotion toward them. For a nuttier flavor, use sesame oil instead of the olive (you may want to go half and half) and replace the peanuts with sesame seeds. Magickally, this opens the creative flow just like Aladdin did by using the power words "Open Sesame!"

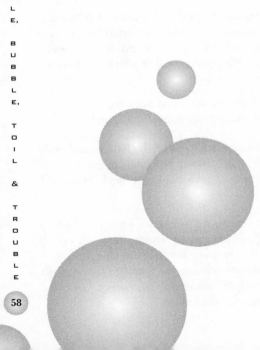

# Snappy-Comeback Snapper

## (SERVES 4)

**I**'ve designed this dish to accent ingenuity in your communications, especially with know-it-alls, wiseacres, and people who are quick to jump into conversations without really having anything worthwhile to say! The yellow tones of the parsnip, carrots, and pepper harmonize with the goal of good oratory skills.

**PREPARING YOUR CAULDRON** Since this spell-recipe focuses on your ability to verbalize in the most effective way possible, begin by either gargling with mint mouthwash or nibbling on a mint leaf. Magickally speaking, mint acts as an overall spiritual tonic and is protective so you can "watch your words." You can also follow this suggestion after consuming your spell-recipe to increase the effect (not to mention keeping your breath fresh).

**COMPONENTS** * 2 medium carrots * 2 medium parsnips * 1 large yellow bell pepper * ³/₄ lb. sweet potato, peeled and cooked tender * ³/₄ cup soy sauce * 2 Tbsp. butter * 4 4–5-oz. red snapper fillets * 2 cups sliced cabbage * 1 Tbsp. white vinegar

**DIRECTIONS** Cut carrots, parsnips, and yellow pepper into thin strips. As you do, focus on anything that you feel is hindering your creative progress and cut that away. The visual effect is improved if you use a vegetable peeler and slice the strips in a motion away from your body.

In a large skillet, sauté the carrots, parsnips, and pepper in the butter. As the carrots and parsnips become tender, add the cabbage along with the vinegar and soy sauce. Coat vegetables evenly (you want the magick to flow evenly into all the components), saying:

> *Parsnips nip criticism at the source, Carrots and cabbage add magickal force.*
> *This spiritual sauce with butter, dipped, Ingenious words flow through my lips!*

When the vegetables are almost cooked, in another pan gently sauté the red snapper fillets in a little cooking oil. If you wish, carve a symbol into the filet using a knife or a toothpick (the image of a pair of lips would be ideal). Brown the fillets evenly until cooked, which also evenly warms and energizes the symbolic representation (about 5 minutes per side depending on thickness).

To serve, place a layer of sweet potatoes on the plate, cover with vegetables, and lay the fish neatly on top. The potatoes create the firm foundation for your spell, while the vegetables inspire, and the fish makes sure you're never at a loss for words! Drizzle a little of the soy-vinegar sauce over all as a finishing touch (remember that the sauce contains your magickal energy too!).

Since this meal is aimed at creative communication, eat very slowly, letting the energy of each bite linger on your tongue. Now, stand up and give a toast or go talk to someone with whom you've been shy. You'll be amazed when your words become as snappy as the snapper!

**ENCHANTING ALTERNATIVES** A black-bean salad on the side inspires creativity in your divinatory efforts, so you can foresee the outcome of your conversations! Mix cooked black beans, sweet corn, diced tomatoes, and a bit of red onion and dress with vinegar, oil, and ground coriander to taste. This is a great salad for people on the go. After all, having a sense of what's ahead helps us avoid a lot of trouble.

# Walk-on-the-Wild-Side
# Mushrooms and Rice

## (SERVES 2–3)

Feel like an adventure, but the rational self keeps getting in the way? Well, put that logic aside momentarily to enjoy some wistful, inventive, and wild living by way of this rice dish.

Nero considered mushrooms food fit for the gods. In Mexico mushrooms represent the ongoing growth process, risk taking, and the inner innovativeness necessary to obtain enlightenment.

**PREPARING YOUR CAULDRON** Walking on the wild side is as much a state of mind as it is actions. Look at the sacred space of your kitchen for a moment and think of something really "wild" to have or do here that you wouldn't normally consider. Purposefully move that object into your view or do that thing to prepare the ambient energy in this space for radical transformation!

**COMPONENTS** * 1 lb. wild mushrooms (your choice) * 1 small onion, chopped * 1 cup pearl onions, peeled * 2 cloves garlic, minced * 1 Tbsp. fresh thyme, chopped * 1 1/4 cup dry red wine * 1 Tbsp. olive oil * salt and pepper * 2 cups cooked wild rice (warm)

**DIRECTIONS** Rinse the mushrooms, drain, and cut them into bite-sized pieces so you can take a real bite out of complacency. Place the mushrooms, onions, garlic, thyme, wine, oil, and salt and pepper to taste in an ovenproof dish and cover it with aluminum foil. The aluminum here serves two functions: practically it keeps the dish from burning or drying; metaphysically it creates a sphere of protection and nurturing in which your magick will warm to perfection.

Marinate the mushrooms at room temperature for 30 minutes, then bake in a 375-degree oven (stirring once every 10 minutes) for about 45 minutes. Remove the aluminum foil and continue cooking for another 30 minutes till the liquid is reduced by half. This is a good point to add an incantation like:

> *Mushrooms and herbs, from nature's grace, Open to me that "wild" place.*
> *The spirit within dreams and believes, Into this dish, my magick weave!*

Serve over a heaping portion of rice, and let the wonderful flavors take you to the wild side of self.

**ENCHANTING ALTERNATIVES** For inventiveness with cash, serve the mushrooms with a crisp salad or over beef.

# CHAPTER 5

# DECISION DISHES

**O**ne of the greatest gifts we have been given in life is the ability to choose. Day to day and moment to moment, our ability to think explicitly and choose according to our conscious mind guides our fate. So it's not surprising that decision dishes need to accent the conscious mind and augment our ability to judge situations clearly.

Some ingredients suited to this task include:

BRAZIL NUTS * CARAWAY SEED * CELERY * COFFEE * DILL *
GRAPES * HAZELNUTS * HONEY * MUSTARD * RAISINS *
ROSEMARY * TEA * TURKEY * WATERCRESS

In looking to the spiritual dimension for these edibles, prepare them when the sun is visible, because the sun represents the light of reason. Sunlight pierces the clouds of uncertainty, illuminates the shadows, and energizes our search for truth no matter where it hides.

To add more symbolic value, consider how the various points in the day might support your magick. For example, if you have to make a decision about a new project, dawn would be the most suitable time. On the other hand, if you're thinking about leaving a situation, dusk is more apt. Noon, of course, is when the sun's logical, conscious nature shines most brightly.

Another alternative is to make several decision dishes and serve them as a buffet. Here you have to "choose" your servings, which is apt for magickal decision-making energy too! Decorate your buffet table with lilacs surrounded by fluorite. Suitable pantry protectors for decision dishes include solar gods and goddesses like Ra (Egypt) and Amaterasu (Japan). Or call on those divine beings known for their wisdom and erudition like Ganesha and Tara (India), Mithra (Persia), and Isis (Egypt).

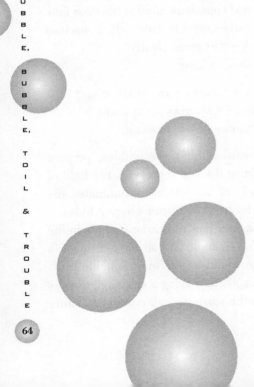

# Crossroads Buns

## (YIELDS 24 BUNS)

Here the symbolism of hot cross buns accents our coming to a crossroad in our lives and having the inner illumination necessary to make the right decision quickly. Traditionally, hot cross buns were made around Easter as a symbol of the sun's return.

**PREPARING YOUR CAULDRON** Put on an item of gold clothing or jewelry, since gold is the color of the conscious mind as well as the sun at its brightest. Add an incantation as you don this item like:

> *Gold to concentrate, options to find,*
> *Give me the focus to make up my mind!*

**COMPONENTS** * 1 1-lb. loaf frozen bread dough * ²/₃ cup raisins * ²/₃ cup chopped hazelnuts * 1 tsp. lemon zest * 2 tsp. orange juice * 1 tsp. vanilla extract * ¹/₂ cup sugar * 1 cup honey

**DIRECTIONS** Follow the directions provided for defrosting and raising the bread dough, keeping your goal in mind all the while. Note that as the dough rises, so does your magickal energy! After the bread rises the first time, knead in all the other ingredients except the honey until evenly blended. Let the dough rise again, then divide dough into 24 portions, roll into balls, and place in a non-stick pan. Bake at 375 degrees for about 15 minutes until golden brown.

Meanwhile, warm the honey so it will drizzle easily. When the buns are cool, pause for a moment and put your hands, palm down, over them, thinking of your choice. Dip your finger in the honey and draw an "X" on each bun, focusing your attention on the center where the two lines touch. In this case, "X" really does mark the spot!

Remember to be considering your decision as you eat the buns. Afterward, write up a pro-and-con list based on the two choices before you and see which one makes more sense!

**ENCHANTING ALTERNATIVES** Use strawberries in place of nuts when making a decision about a romantic relationship, or red currants for decisions related to health or finances.

# Slice-of-Life Hazelnut Piecrust

## (YIELDS 1 9-INCH PIECRUST)

**D**ecision making always creates a unique slice of life, and our final choices determine the size and flavor of that slice as well as how it's served! For this spell-recipe, we turn to brandy to put a fire under the process and hazelnuts for good luck!

**PREPARING YOUR CAULDRON** This crust is meant to act like a womb for your magick, so fill it with any type of pie filling that symbolizes the area of your life in which a decision is pending. For example, if you are thinking of moving, you might make a pecan filling (pecans are associated with the air element, and thus movement). Or, to decide which expenses to eliminate in your budget, use a quince filling (a fruit associated with the earth element and happy outcomes).

**COMPONENTS** * 7 honey graham crackers, crushed * ½ cup hazelnuts * 2 Tbsp. brown sugar * ¼ cup butter * 2 Tbsp. hazelnut brandy or liqueur

**DIRECTIONS** Grease a 9-inch pie pan lightly with vegetable oil. Draw an image of the area of your life in which a decision is needed in the oil too, if you wish (e.g., draw a house when you're trying to choose a new residence). Place the graham crackers, hazelnuts, and brown sugar in a blender and blend until ground. This blends magickal energy, whips up a little extra power, and also breaks down the barriers between you and making a sound decision. Scrape the mixture out of the blender into a bowl, add the butter and brandy, and mix by hand until evenly distributed. Press this evenly into the pie pan and bake in a 350-degree oven for 10 minutes. Fill as desired.

As you slice this "life" pie, remember that the act of slicing opens and activates the flow of magick, so that would be an ideal time to add an incantation that empowers your effort, like:

*When opened with my kitchen knife, manifest a slice of life!*
*To banish any reservations, I bite into this sweet sensation!*

**ENCHANTING ALTERNATIVES** Top your pie with candied hazelnuts or a hearty portion of whipping cream. The cream accents gentle acceptance of whatever choice you make.

# Nutty Sweet Confections

## (YIELDS 1 CUP)

**F**ollowing the example provided in European folklore, we're adding hazelnuts to this spell-recipe to help us apply knowledge wisely, including making difficult choices with good humor as a helpmate.

**PREPARING YOUR CAULDRON** What area of your life is being affected by the decision you are trying to make? Write down some key words that describe it, then consider what other components might be used in this spell-recipe to support that goal. For example, add almonds to the blend if your choice has to do with finances or health, coconut for spiritual matters, and pecans if the decision is employment related.

**COMPONENTS** * 1 cup water * 1 ¼ cup sugar * ½ cup hazelnuts * ⅓ cup Brazil nuts * 1 Tbsp. butter

**DIRECTIONS** Simmer the water and sugar until the sugar is dissolved. Stir nuts into the sugar water, then transfer them to a nonstick baking pan using a slotted spoon. Bake in a 350-degree oven for 15 minutes until brown. Melt the butter and pour it over the nuts, making sure to turn and coat them evenly, saying:

> *Nuts and butter, nuts and butter, Grant to me all the logic I can muster.*
> *Turn and change, remove all fear, By magick and will, my choice make clear!*

Finally, put the nuts on waxed paper to cool (they get crisp upon cooling). Store in an airtight container to preserve the energy and crispness.

Nibble as desired, especially when you want to consciously, logically mull over several options.

**ENCHANTING ALTERNATIVES** Store with dried fruit pieces. Blend in apple slices for wisdom, pineapple for decisions regarding guests in your home, dates when you need to be firm in your choice, and papaya for love-related issues.

# Make-Up-Your-Mind French Toast

## (SERVES 2)

When you're facing a hectic day filled with numerous choices, this breakfast is perfect! It provides you with energy, improved concentration, and all the right ingredients to make the best possible decisions all day long.

**PREPARING YOUR CAULDRON** Breakfast is the most important meal of the day, especially when there are difficult choices looming on the horizon. So look at your breakfast as a mini-ritual. Add a tall glass of orange juice for healthy outlooks, pouring a little out your window or door by way of an offering. Light a candle to light the way toward positive change, and consider saying a brief prayer over your food so that all the magick you're placing in it is released in the best possible way.

**COMPONENTS** * ½ cup vanilla ice cream * 2 eggs * ¼ cup ground hazelnuts * 1 Tbsp. rum flavoring * ⅛ tsp. cinnamon * 4 slices raisin bread * butter and syrup (topping)

**DIRECTIONS** Melt the ice cream and mix thoroughly with eggs, nuts, flavoring, and cinnamon. As you do, visualize any barriers between you and your final choice melting neatly away. Dip the bread slices into this mixture so that they are evenly coated on both sides (this surrounds the bread with your magick). Fry these gently on low. After the first turn, use a toothpick or knife to etch a magickal symbol on the sides, and let the remaining frying process heat up your magic. With each turn of the bread, add an incantation like:

*Bread for sound foundations, cinnamon for energy.*
*To make my choice, this spell is freed!*

Serve with butter and syrup.

**ENCHANTING ALTERNATIVES** Change the type of bread so it more closely resembles the question at hand. For example, wheat bread and cornbread relate well to money, sourdough bread represents a decision that's somewhat distasteful to make, and white bread symbolizes a common, everyday choice that for some reason has you stumped.

# Telltale Turkey

## (SERVES 1)

The turkey and mustard in this spell-recipe help with fact-finding, so that you'll have the information and insight necessary to make a good choice. The maple syrup brings abundant joy with that decision.

**PREPARING YOUR CAULDRON** Fact-finding has both conscious and intuitive elements to it. You need to look logically, but also trust your gut instincts to lead you in the right direction. Consequently, time this spell-recipe so you're putting the basic components together at midnight, dawn, on New Year's, or any other date or time that's balanced on a hinge (midnight and dawn are between darkness and light, New Year's is between two years, etc.). Wear black and white clothing while you're preparing this spell-recipe, so that your final decision will be as clear as "black and white." One easy choice here would be one black and one white sock. Since these go on your feet, they also help represent a decision that has good foundations!

**COMPONENTS** * 1 6–8-oz. turkey breast steak * ¼ cup wine vinegar * ¼ cup sesame oil * 2 Tbsp. soy sauce * 1 tsp. *each* salt, ginger, and anise * 2 Tbsp. brown sugar * 2 orange slices * ¼ cup maple syrup * ¼ cup white cooking wine * 2 Tbsp. spicy mustard * 1 tsp. butter

**DIRECTIONS** Pierce the turkey steak with a fork to pierce any misconceptions or illusions you have with regard to any aspect of this decision. Marinate it in a blend of the vinegar, oil, soy sauce, salt, ginger, anise, and the juice of the two orange slices for 6 hours in the refrigerator, turning it regularly, saying:

*Turkey and salt, uncertainty halt.*
*Ginger and juice, my decision deduce!*

Meanwhile, create the glaze by mixing the syrup, wine, mustard, and butter together in a saucepan. Set this aside and use it to brush on the turkey while grilling it. Generally speaking, it will take about 30 minutes to cook the turkey completely on a medium-heat grill, basting every 7 minutes for even coating. If you have the ability to smoke things on your grill, add hickory chips into the blend for an amazingly rich taste. Garnish with additional orange wedges.

Don't be surprised if your mind starts rolling with fresh outlooks about the matter at hand shortly after dinner!

**ENCHANTING ALTERNATIVES** Substitute lemon juice for the orange in this spell-recipe to improve mental clarity.

# CHAPTER 6

# KNOWLEDGE NOSHES
# AND EDUCATION RATIONS

**L**ife is a never-ending learning process. Typically, something always comes along to surprise you, as if the script for living was written by Murphy himself.

Even so, there are many times when we want to feel more mentally "on" and in control. For example, if you're in school (at any age) a little magick can bolster your memory skills. Or if you want to improve your talents for your chosen profession, you'll want to eat a bunch of knowledge foods. Here are some of the components that will help get you started:

APPLES * BEANS AND SEEDS * CARAWAY SEED * CELERY *
CITRUS FRUITS * COFFEE * DILL * FIGS * GRAPES * GREENS *
HOT FOODS AND SPICES * MEAT * MINT * NUTMEG *
ROOT VEGETABLES * ROSEMARY * SAVORY * TEA *
WALNUTS * WATERCRESS

Like conscious-mind foods, education rations should be prepared in the light of day (unless the subject matter at hand is of an esoteric or intuitive nature like magick and philosophy). Decorate your table with sprigs of rosemary, whose aroma strengthens memory, or bits of aventurine, a stone that improves mental power. For pantry protectors consider Chin Chia (China), Balder (Scandinavia), Benten (Japan), and Ihi (Tahiti).

# Kernels of Knowledge

### (SERVES 2–3)

The symbolism in this dish is designed to help you internalize tidbits of knowledge that, like well-tended seeds, will eventually grow and bear fruit in reality.

**PREPARING YOUR CAULDRON** Take a moment and consider exactly what type of learning you're attempting. Use the type of seed or bean that best suits your goal. For example, use yellow beans to learn how to communicate better, or all white beans when you're learning about spiritual matters. Black-eyed peas might be used for learning psychic arts (e.g., to "see" better), green beans for learning how to balance the budget, red beans when you need to be more informed about a relationship, and black beans when you need to put down solid foundations for your education.

**COMPONENTS** * 1 cup sweet corn, drained * 1 cup baby peas, drained * 1 cup black-eyed peas, precooked * 1 tsp. sesame seeds * 1 Tbsp. sunflower seeds * 1 Tbsp. olive oil * 6 soft taco shells * chili powder or other hot spices, to taste * sour cream (garnish)

**DIRECTIONS** Warm the corn, peas, and seeds together with half of the olive oil in a small pan on low. Meanwhile, lightly oil the tacos and place them on a flat-top grill to warm. You can make these crunchy if you prefer, but I like them soft for wrapping around the ingredients so that it creates a "womb" in which to nurture the magickal energy you're creating. Paint the sour cream onto the taco shell in a design that represents your goal. While you sprinkle the corn mixture with whatever Mexican-style spices you enjoy, add an incantation like:

> *Within this shell the magick burns,*
> *Help me in my quest to learn!*

Note that if you don't overfill the taco shells, these make a great study food, so that you can snack on your magick while accomplishing your goal!

**ENCHANTING ALTERNATIVES** Add grape tomatoes when you need more enthusiasm for learning, onions to keep distractions at bay and increase your physical energy and attentiveness, or refried beans to better comprehend something you've already learned. You can also add other herbs or vegetables into this blend for sympathetic energy and flavorful changes. In particular, thyme inspires balance in the learning process (whatever you put in is what you'll get back), marjoram inspires a sense of peace about learning a new subject, dill provides mental focus, and chopped beefsteak tomatoes bring positive learning experiences your way.

# Grounded Meatballs

## (SERVES 4–5)

**W**hen you find your mind straying and your ability to focus completely blown by other matters, these meatballs bring you firmly back down to earth—get grounded in ground round! They also make a nice post-ritual feast that inspires a firm reconnection to the temporal realm.

**PREPARING YOUR CAULDRON** The best place to eat these meatballs is on the ground, so set up a picnic-style eating spot either outdoors or somewhere in the house on the floor. Sit here for a few minutes before preparing the spell-recipe to center and focus your will (which also helps support the goal of the spell). Take three deep breaths (for body-mind-spirit working in symmetry), then go into the kitchen being fully connected to the earth element, which encourages foundations.

**COMPONENTS** * ¹/₂ cup herbed bread crumbs * ²/₃ cup milk * 1 small onion, finely diced * ¹/₂ lb. ground round * ¹/₄ lb. ground pork * 1 egg * 1 tsp. *each* garlic and onion powder * 1 tsp. Worcestershire sauce * pinch of nutmeg * salt and pepper, to taste * olive oil (for frying)

**DIRECTIONS** Mix all ingredients together thoroughly. Form the meat into balls 1 to 1 ¹/₂ inches in diameter. Remember to keep your goal in mind while you shape the meat into balls (which is the symbol of completion!). Gently brown the meatballs in olive oil, saying an incantation like this three times (again, to stress the body-mind-spirit connection):

*Mind wander no more. Come, Focus, and Aim!*
*By this spell, solid foundations I claim!*

Bake the energized meatballs in the oven at 300 degrees for about 25 minutes. This has the additional benefit of letting excess fat drain out of the meat.

Serve with noodles, or as an appetizer by themselves.

**ENCHANTING ALTERNATIVES** Put a slice of garlic into the center of each meatball to safeguard your knowledge. The garlic slices can be eaten with the meatballs or placed inside warm bread rolls with butter as a side dish. Another alternative is to shape the meatballs like an eye, which represents knowledge, wisdom, and insight. Note to vegetarians: Use an equal quantity of drained and finely ground tofu instead of meat in this dish. I suggest also grinding up a bit of carrot with it (a root vegetable) for the foundational energy desired.

# Candied Clarity Strips

## (YIELDS 2 PINTS)

**W**hen you're tired of hitting the books, and your eyes feel ready to fall out of your head, the aroma and flavor of citrus fruit in this dish will refresh your tired mind. The preserved nature of these treats helps you confidently retain what you learn and compartmentalize it for when it is needed later.

**PREPARING YOUR CAULDRON** Soak a clean washcloth in cool water into which you've placed a drop or two of citrus oil (grapefruit is one that maintains continuity with this spell-recipe). Dab this gently counterclockwise on your face, saying,

*Weariness away, heed the words I say,*
*Exhaustion bind, refresh my mind!*

**COMPONENTS** * 1 large pink grapefruit * 1 large orange * 1 1/2 cups water * 2/3 cup sugar * 2 Tbsp. light corn syrup * 1/2 tsp. vanilla extract

**DIRECTIONS** Remove the peels from the grapefruit and orange very carefully (think of this as removing weariness from your shoulders). Cut the peels into 1/2-inch strips. Scrape off as much of the white pith as possible, then boil the strips in water for 10 minutes until tender. Drain.

In another large saucepan bring the water, sugar, corn syrup, and vanilla to a boil. Stir clockwise often so the sugar is completely dissolved as you invoke increased energy with an incantation like:

*Oranges of earth, with grapefruit bind,*
*Bring to me a crystal-clear mind!*

Simmer the citrus strips in this syrup for 20–25 minutes until the citrus is somewhat translucent and the syrup is very thick. Lay the strips on waxed paper to cool and dry. Store in an airtight container in the refrigerator for the longest shelf life.

Once completely cooled, enjoy a tiny bite and breathe deeply. Let your weariness fall away and claim clear-mindedness! Serve as a snack when studying or as an after-dinner treat before you hit the books.

**ENCHANTING ALTERNATIVES** As the strips are cooling, sprinkle them with a mixture of sugar and cinnamon or ginger, both of which add extra energy to your magick. Stack one orange strip on top of one grapefruit strip for very nice visual appeal.

# Steady-Study Crunchy Munchies

## (SERVES 1)

**S**imple is often better, especially when you need to direct your attention to the work at hand. For this spell-recipe I've turned to crunchy food to help you keep one foot on the ground, your energy high, and your resolution sure.

**PREPARING YOUR CAULDRON** Steep two pinches of fresh rosemary in 2 Tbsp. of good olive oil, warming until the oil smells heavily of the rosemary. Dab this on the items you'll be using to study, saying:

> *In this oil my magick burns,*
> *Help me in my quest to learn!*

Note: Unused rosemary oil can be stored for up to six months in a dark, airtight container. Use it on your pulse points or books anytime you want to improve your memory.

**COMPONENTS** * ¼ cup finely diced apple * ½ tsp. finely chopped rosemary * ¼ cup softened cream cheese * celery stalks

**DIRECTIONS** Mix the apple and rosemary with the softened cream cheese and fill the celery stalks or dip the stalks into it. Nibble while you're studying! You'll find the crunching and the magick keep you from getting distracted.

**ENCHANTING ALTERNATIVES** Eliminate the apple and rosemary, and instead add dill to the cream cheese with a little salt. The magickal results are the same, but the flavor is dramatically different. Or chop up fig instead of apple, as it was under a fig tree that Buddha achieved enlightenment.

## CHAPTER 7

# EMPLOYMENT EDIBLES

There is nothing worse than being stuck in a job you don't like, one where you feel inadequate, one that doesn't meet the bills, or one where no one seems to appreciate your efforts. So when you're trying to improve your position, by getting either a new job, a transfer, or perhaps a promotion, employment edibles are a good place to start. In essence, you're going to consume all the qualities you feel you need for success.

Some ingredients suited to this general category include:

ALFALFA * ALMONDS * BASIL * BAY LEAVES * CASHEWS *
CHAMOMILE * CINNAMON * CLOVES * DILL * GINGER * GRAPES *
MAPLE SYRUP * MEAT * MINT * NUTMEG * OATS * ORANGES *
PECANS * PINEAPPLE * POMEGRANATES * RADISHES *
SALT * WHEAT

Decorate your table with pine fronds, which will attract money your way, while neatly cleansing any negativity that's lingering around. A good crystal to augment this energy is agate for self-improvements, or specifically an eye agate to protect your job. For pantry protectors, look to gods and goddesses who can influence fate such as Cosa (Africa), Fatum (Rome), Laima (Latvia), and Shai (Egypt).

# Turn-It-Around Pineapple Cake

## (SERVES 6)

The whole purpose of this cake is to literally turn the business world on its ear (upside down) with your aptitude! The pineapple in the spell-recipe also makes people more congenial toward you (in early American decorating schemes, the pineapple represented hospitality and welcome).

**PREPARING YOUR CAULDRON** In what line of work are you employed? Think of a simple emblem that represents that work. For example, someone who works in computers might use a square (the computer screen). Pattern that image in the pan using maraschino cherries before the pineapple is placed in it to literally bake your intention into the cake.

**COMPONENTS** * 6 slices pineapple, canned or fresh * 6 Tbsp. butter * 3/4 cup packed dark brown sugar * 1 1/2 cups flour * 2 tsp. baking powder * 1/4 tsp. salt * 6 Tbsp. unsalted butter, softened * 1 cup granulated sugar * 2 large eggs * 1 tsp. vanilla extract * 1 Tbsp. rum flavoring * 1/2 cup pineapple juice * maraschino cherries (optional)

**DIRECTIONS** In a large skillet, melt the butter, slowly adding the brown sugar to it. Toss the pineapple slices liberally in this mixture, saying:

*Sweet hospitality, open opportunity's doors to me!*

Place the pineapple slices evenly in the bottom of a well-oiled 9-inch round cake pan (these go *over* the cherries if you've chosen to use them). Set aside.

Cream softened butter and sugar, then add eggs, flavorings, and pineapple juice. Add dry ingredients and mix well. Pour evenly over the top of the pineapple slices, then bake at 350 degrees for 45 minutes. Let cool for about 7 minutes. Loosen the sides of the cake and flip out onto a serving platter. As you turn out the cake, say:

*With a turn of a cake, a turn of luck, a turn of fate,*
*Let my talents flow, constraints abate!*

Remove any pineapple or cherries that don't come out of the cake pan and put on top of the cake. If you wish, drizzle with sweet cream or rum-flavored whipped cream, both of which sustain the magick you've created, adding a slightly protective dimension.

**ENCHANTING ALTERNATIVES** For more personal clarity, intermingle the pineapple slices with peeled oranges sliced in the same manner as the pineapple. For wisdom in your interview, add thinly sliced apples or peaches.

# Resumé Radishes

## (YIELDS ¾ CUP DIPPING SAUCE)

Nibble on these zesty snacks while you're updating your resumé. Before you know it, you'll be offered that dream job (and it will be a "hot" one!).

**PREPARING YOUR CAULDRON** Honest effort is one of the greatest magicks in the world. So before creating this dish, collect several newspapers that carry employment listings. Have these ready to peruse while you eat or just shortly thereafter, send out those resumés, and follow up on each diligently!

**COMPONENTS** * ¼ cup sour cream * ¼ cup salad dressing (any kind) * ¼ cup cream cheese, softened * 1 Tbsp. minced fresh chives * 1 Tbsp. dried dill weed * ¼ tsp. hot sauce * ¼ tsp. Worcestershire sauce * 1 bag or bunch radishes (cleaned)

**DIRECTIONS** Place all the ingredients except radishes in a mixing bowl and blend liberally, saying:

*The magick begins with resumés sent,*
*Bring to me secure employment!*

Repeat the incantation as many times as you wish, but four is a good number for establishing foundations. Pour the dip into a dish (perhaps a green one for prosperity) and dip in radishes as desired (just don't spill any on your resumé!). Store excess in an airtight container, which also preserves your magick.

BUBBLE, BUBBLE, TOIL & TROUBLE

Now go get some ads and intuitively mail out your resumé. Eat a couple of snacks just before these go in the mail. Your phone will be ringing off the hook within two weeks.

**ENCHANTING ALTERNATIVES** This dip also goes well with bread and other vegetables. Combine it with carrots for improved instincts in your interviews, celery for a better self-image, or broccoli and cauliflower to protect the jobs you're most interested in until you get the chance to at least present yourself.

Alternatively, choose the type of salad dressing you use so it corresponds to your employment goals. A cucumber dressing, for example, represents a health-related profession, and a cumin-flavored dressing symbolizes a safety-oriented profession because of its protective power.

# Fame-and-Fortune Shrimp

## (SERVES 4 AS AN APPETIZER)

Shellfish symbolize profuseness, in this case financial abundance. Shrimp also keeps your psychic self honed so you recognize good opportunities wherever and whenever they present themselves. Cloves promote a sense of rapport with co-workers, bosses, or interviewers.

**PREPARING YOUR CAULDRON** Dress for success! Put on something that represents a personal victory in whatever employment matter is at hand. For example, if you're going for a promotion and you'd use or wear something different in your new job, get that item or don those clothes before beginning your spell-recipe. What we wear changes the way we feel, which in turn improves the outcome of our magick!

**COMPONENTS** * 2 ½ cups water * ¾ cup white wine * ¼ lemon * ¼ orange * ½ Tbsp. salt * 1 bay leaf * ¼-inch slice ginger root, pounded * 1 tsp. red pepper flakes (optional) * 1 bunch green onions, chopped * 2 lbs. large shrimp * 2 tsp. white wine vinegar * 1 Tbsp. lemon juice * 2 Tbsp. orange juice * ½ tsp. ginger * ¼ cup olive oil * 1 tsp. diced garlic * sugar, salt, pepper, to taste

**DIRECTIONS** Using a large soup kettle (symbolically a cauldron), boil the water with the next eight ingredients (wine through onions) for 10 minutes. Turn down the water to a low rolling boil. Add the shrimp and cook for 4–8 minutes until pink. This is a good time to add an incantation like:

*With the water's motion*
*I claim my promotion!*

Strain the shrimp. If you wish, you can use the stock as the base for a precharged financial fish soup (refrigerate and use within 48 hours or discard).

In a large food storage container, mix together the vinegar, juices, oil, ginger, and garlic, remembering to stir clockwise to engender positive energy. Sprinkle with a pinch of sugar and salt and pepper to bring out the richness of these flavors. Marinate the shrimp in this mixture for 12 hours in the refrigerator. Strain again and serve cold so that you will keep a cool head no matter what employment opportunities come your way.

Eat just before going into an important meeting, prior to a review, or on the day of an interview (note: follow with a breath mint, to keep communications fresh!).

**ENCHANTING ALTERNATIVES** If you're going for a really "hot" job, warm the shrimp, skewered together with orange pieces, pineapple, or onion and pepper slices, on a grill.

If you think there might be some kind of deception going on at the workplace or in the interview process, use crab in this spell-recipe instead of shrimp (crab symbolizes dishonesty, which you overcome by eating it!).

Substitute clams for shrimp in instances where you're hoping to illustrate strong written and verbal skills. In shamanic lore, clams were assistants to Spider Woman, who invented the alphabet.

# Power Pancakes

## (SERVES 4)

**O**ats are among the most popular foods representing providence and prosperity. To this base we've added energy herbs and some fruit to open the doors for abundant opportunities and/or options in your career.

**PREPARING YOUR CAULDRON** Since one of the chief goals of this breakfast is providing a physical and mental boost for the day, place three candles on your kitchen table: one red (for physical energy), one yellow (for the conscious mind), and one in your favorite color to represent the self. Light them, saying:

> *The flame of power I claim [red candle].*
> *The flame of insight and perception I claim [yellow candle].*
> *The flame of self-confidence I claim [your candle].*

Leave the candles burning while you prepare this dish.

**COMPONENTS** * 2 cups oatmeal * ½ cup all-purpose flour * 2 Tbsp. granulated sugar * 2 Tbsp. brown sugar * 1 tsp. baking soda * 1 tsp. baking powder * ½ tsp. salt * ¼ tsp. cinnamon * ¼ tsp. ground cloves * 2 cups milk * ½ cup strawberry juice * 2 large eggs * ¼ cup butter, melted * 1 tsp. vanilla extract * cooking oil

**DIRECTIONS** In a large bowl combine all the dry ingredients, making sure the spices, baking powder, and baking soda are well integrated. Slowly add the milk and juice to make a thick batter. Beat the two eggs separately and then fold them in. Whisk in butter and vanilla, repeating an adaptation of the previous verbal component while you stir. For example, chant:

*Power I claim, Perception I claim,*
*Confidence I claim, Insecurity tamed!*

Chill slightly for a thicker batter.

Meanwhile, prepare a skillet or griddle with cooking oil. Pour out ¼ cupfuls of the batter on the frying surface at a time. Wait for bubbles to appear evenly in the surface of the pancakes (this is a good time to etch a dollar sign in them for prosperity), then turn over and cook the other side.

Serve with real maple syrup so those opportunities flow as liberally as the maple trees in spring!

**ENCHANTING ALTERNATIVES** Instead of syrup, serve the pancakes with preserves to preserve your job, or with a variety of fresh fruit to open a wide variety of opportunities.

# CHAPTER 8

# FORTUNE FOODS

**W**ho doesn't periodically wish for a little more luck? Whether it's finding a five-dollar bill on the street or running into an important contact at just the right moment, a little serendipity makes life a lot more pleasant (not to mention more fun!). Fortune foods help us internalize the energy of luck, so we carry it with us and in turn attract more our way.

Some foods are naturally aligned with luck depending on when we eat them or how we prepare them. For example, stirring Christmas pudding is thought to bring luck, as is eating wedding cake. Similarly, people in China eat rice on their birthday for good fortune the way we have cake.

Other ingredients known for their fortuitous energy include:

ALLSPICE * BAMBOO SHOOTS * BANANAS * BEER *
BLACK-EYED PEAS * CABBAGE * CHAMPAGNE * COCONUT *
COLESLAW * FISH * HAZELNUTS * KUMQUATS * MINCEMEAT *
NOODLES * NUTMEG * ORANGES * PEARS * PINEAPPLE *
POMEGRANATES * RED BEANS * RICE * SUGAR * TEA * WINE

For the magickal element, prepare fortune foods in numbers that match your lucky number, or improve their symbolism by adding colors you consider lucky. Decorate the table with bluebells, roses, or violets accented by jet and tiger's eye stones. Remember to pass all foods sunward to keep luck moving in the right direction. And, finally, pantry protectors who preside over good fortune include Ebisu (Japan), Fortuna (Italy), Ganesa (India), and Salida (Germany).

# Fortui-Tea

## (SERVES 6)

Ｉf the flow of good luck could be easily poured into a glass, this beverage would be the perfect choice! It has all the right herbs and spices, along with some champagne to uplift the energy in the whole blend and rum to protect your luck when it arrives.

**PREPARING YOUR CAULDRON** According to folklore, putting the tea and sugar into your serving pot before the water or milk ensures good luck. Give this a try while adding an incantation like:

*Sugar brings luck so very sweet, My every need, this magick meets.*
*Soon ill fortunes shall all abate, With tea to transform my future fate!*

**COMPONENTS** * 2 1/4 cups water * 1/3 cup sugar * 1/4 cup brown sugar * 1 Tbsp. chopped ginger * 8 cloves * 8 allspice berries * 2 vanilla tea bags * 2 orange tea bags * 1 bottle (750 ml.) dry champagne * 1/4 cup rum (optional)

**DIRECTIONS** Boil the water. Place the sugar, spices, and tea bags into a kettle or pot, and pour in the boiled water. Steep for 10 minutes until heady with aroma. Whisper your wishes into the steam, so it rises to the four winds to express your need. Strain into a punch bowl (perhaps one that's your lucky color) and add the champagne and rum. Serve over crushed ice.

**ENCHANTING ALTERNATIVES** Vary the kind of tea bags to direct luck to the area where you most need it, like using mint instead of orange for financial luck. You can also use honey instead of sugar to stimulate more serendipity.

# Fishin' for Luck

## (SERVES 2)

Need a fortunate windfall or a dramatic change in fate? This spell-recipe produces the energy necessary to help that happen. According to an Arabian proverb, pitch a lucky man into the Nile and he will come up with a fish in his mouth! In this case we're one step ahead of the game because we have the fish already (and it doesn't have to be Friday)!

**PREPARING YOUR CAULDRON** It's fun to do a fishing motif for this spell-recipe. Wear a fisherman's cap. Make a makeshift fishing line out of a wooden spoon and some thread. On the end of that thread place an edible item that represents the area of your life in which more luck is needed. For example, if you need financial luck, use something green. Dip periodically in the marinade to catch luck, saying:

> *Oil smoothes the way for change, All my luck—rearrange!*
> *Here, surrounded in fine wine, I claim my fate, good luck is mine.*

If the item you've chosen needs to be cooked, cook it with the fish. Otherwise, eat it before starting the spell-recipe. This adjusts your aura to better accept the energies you're about to create.

**COMPONENTS** * ½ lb. white fish fillet strips * 2 Tbsp. olive oil * 1 Tbsp. chopped garlic * 1 cup diced red and white onion * pinch of oregano * ¼ cup wine vinegar * ¼ cup cooking wine * pinch of sugar * ¼ cup milk * seasoned flour for dredging

**DIRECTIONS** Sauté the garlic and onion in the olive oil, then move to a marinating dish. Add the oregano, vinegar, your choice of cooking wine, and sugar. Marinate fish in this mixture for 2–3 hours in the refrigerator. Drain.

Dip the fish in milk, which nurtures your magic, then dredge in flour seasoned with salt and pepper. Fry in a nonstick pan until golden brown. Note that after the first turn you can etch an image into the surface of the fish to energize your focus further.

Drain on paper towels and serve with a hearty portion of rice (especially good for luck with money) or potatoes (which provide solid foundations in which your fortune can take root).

**ENCHANTING ALTERNATIVES** Use white wine in this spell-recipe if you were born under the sign of Aries, want luck with friendship, or need assistance with a difficult change. Use a red wine if you were born under Scorpio or need luck with health or a leadership matter.

# Sweet Serendipity Sauce

## (YIELDS 1 CUP)

When you want a nice warm blend that brings out serendipity in a bold and zesty way, make this sauce and enjoy it over some vanilla ice cream to savor sweet success!

**PREPARING YOUR CAULDRON** Find a dish that's your lucky color to serve this spell-recipe in. Or put on a shirt or some other item of clothing that really energizes you. Remember, luck has a lot to do with your personal vibes—if you feel down, you tend to attract negativity instead of the positive energy you want.

**COMPONENTS** * 1/2 cup mincemeat * 1/3 cup sugar * 1/2 cup orange juice * 1/4 cup ginger brandy * 1 tsp. cinnamon * 2 Tbsp. whipping cream

**DIRECTIONS** Combine the first five ingredients in a medium saucepan, saying:

> *Mincemeat to bless this lucky treat, Sugar to make the spell complete.*
> *Orange juice for healthy thoughts and ways, Brandy to protect me all my days.*
> *And last, a pinch of cinnamon flick, So that fortune starts to stick!*

Warm over medium heat, stirring clockwise until the sugar is completely dissolved. Slowly raise the temperature so the liquid boils, then simmer on low until the sauce reduces and thickens to the consistency of maple syrup. Remove from the heat, add cream, and then chill and use as desired.

**ENCHANTING ALTERNATIVES** To make this sauce even more fortune-bearing, serve it on Christmas Day. To direct the energy of the sauce into specific areas of your life, use numeric or flavor correspondences for the ice cream. For example, if you want luck in a partnership, serve the sauce over two small scoops of ice cream. If you want luck with money, serve the sauce over orange sherbet.

# Open-Sesame Spaghetti

## (SERVES 3–4)

**M**ake this dish and, like Aladdin, watch opportunity open before you.

**PREPARING YOUR CAULDRON** It was quite common in Arabic regions to have a special prayer rug that people took with them everywhere. If you have a small, pretty rug around the house, bring it into your kitchen. Sit comfortably, take several deep breaths, and pray to Spirit in whatever manner feels comfortable, especially a god or goddess under whose dominion luck and fate come! Express your needs and ask for a blessing on your spell-recipe, then stand on the rug while you cook to keep that energy flowing!

**COMPONENTS** * 1 Tbsp. chopped garlic * 2 Tbsp. sesame oil * 1 ½ Tbsp. soy sauce * scant Tbsp. rice vinegar * ¼ cup cashews, chopped * 2 Tbsp. sesame seeds * ¼ cup water * ½ lb. thin spaghetti * sesame sticks (garnish)

**DIRECTIONS** Sauté the garlic in sesame oil. Transfer to a blender, adding soy, vinegar, cashews, sesame seeds, and water. Blend until smooth, saying:

*Open Sesame! Open the way!*
*I need fast changes, bring good luck today!*

Leave mixture at room temperature while you prepare the spaghetti to personally desired tenderness. Toss the drained spaghetti noodles with the sauce (to stir up good fortune) and garnish with sesame sticks.

**ENCHANTING ALTERNATIVES** Add some cooked chicken marinated with soy and ginger for luck with your well-being, or pork for luck in the way people perceive you.

# Chance-Enhancing Coleslaw

## (SERVES 2)

**E**ver catch yourself saying "If I only had the chance . . . "? Well, let this dish implore the fates on your behalf!

B U B B L E , B U B B L E , T O I L & T R O U B L E

**PREPARING YOUR CAULDRON** Chance is often as much a matter of personal ingenuity as it is a matter of luck. So if you can prepare this dish at noon for mental clarity and perception, all the better. Also, light a yellow candle in the area where you're working (for creativity), saying:

*The light of hope, be with me, The light of awareness and insight, fill me, The light of protection, surround me, The light of luck, be mine.*

**COMPONENTS** * 1¼ cups shredded green cabbage * ¼ cup shredded carrot * ¼ cup shredded red cabbage * ½ cup baby peas or snow peas * ¼ cup springwater sprouts (optional) * 2 tsp. wine vinegar * ½ tsp. dry mustard * ½ tsp. ground ginger * 2 Tbsp. sesame oil * 1 tsp. soy sauce

**DIRECTIONS** Place the first five ingredients in a large bowl and toss. This is a good time to repeat your incantation to reinforce the magick you began. In a separate container blend the remaining ingredients to create a zesty dressing that jumps with lucky energy. Make sure everything is well blended, then pour as much as you wish over the cabbage mixture.

Eat with hope in your heart and watch the options that open to you in the next few days, or even hours!

**ENCHANTING ALTERNATIVES** Increase the proportion of red cabbage for luck in love, or the carrot for good fortune with fertility-related matters.

## CHAPTER 9

# HAPPINESS HELPINGS

The kitchen cauldron should always be filled to overflowing with joy, contentment, and fulfillment. Any foods prepared with a happy heart will be contagious and have positive effects on everyone partaking.

Some of the foods believed to lift spirits and return gladness include:

APPLES * APRICOTS * BARLEY * BEER * BUBBLY BEVERAGES *
CELERY * CHERRIES * CHOCOLATE * CUCUMBERS * CUMIN *
HONEY * LEMONS * LETTUCE * MARJORAM * MILK * MINT *
OLIVES * OREGANO * PEACHES * QUINCE * RASPBERRIES *
SAFFRON * WINE

Important: you should *enjoy* the foods you use to bring joy into your life! Otherwise you're undermining the entire energy of the spell-recipe (a sour face makes for a similarly sour disposition!).

Lay out your happiness helpings in whimsical ways that bring a smile to the face (like patterning sliced hot dogs into the shape of a smile). Stir ingredients counterclockwise when banishing the blues, or clockwise when you wish to inspire felicity. Decorate your table with amethyst crystals, morning glory, and hyacinth, all of which bring joy and peace into the home. For pantry protectors turn to Bast and Bes (Egypt), Comus (Rome), or Marimba (Africa).

# Brisket Full of Blessings

## (SERVES 4–5)

Need just a little blessing to make everything better? This dish does the trick! Both the honey and the apple juice in this spell-recipe evoke healthy joy. Ginger energizes everything, while garlic protects your happiness, and vanilla inspires love.

**COMPONENTS** * 1 2 ½-lb. lean beef brisket * 1 cup honey * ½ cup apple juice * 1 tsp. ground ginger * 1 tsp. vanilla extract * 1 tsp. finely chopped garlic

**PREPARING YOUR CAULDRON** Early in the day (dawn is ideal as the time of hope) put the brisket in a large pot and cover with salted water. Cover and bring to a low rolling boil and simmer for 5 hours, adding water as necessary to keep the meat covered with liquid. Each hour, turn the brisket, adding an incantation to get the magick moving like:

> *Beef bubble and turn, he magick burns, Within my heart and soul.*
> *Water to cleanse, joy to impart, Make my spirit whole!*

Check the brisket; the meat should be flaky (magickally speaking, this breaks apart negativity and lets the magickal baste saturate the meat). Transfer the brisket to a baking pan and score the top of the brisket with X marks (or any other symbols that represent your goal).

In a small saucepan, warm the honey, apple juice, and spices together until the honey is completely dissolved. Pour over the brisket, making sure it gets into the cracks, focusing on your goal and saying:

*Honey so fine, with happiness shine*
*Here, magick bind, true joy be mine!*

Cover with aluminum foil and bake at 300 degrees for 30–45 minutes so the honey makes a glaze. Turn the brisket once during cooking so both sides of the meat receive some of the magickal glaze.

Slice thinly and serve. Watch your mood improve with each bite!

**ENCHANTING ALTERNATIVES** Change the fruit juice in this spell-recipe to mirror your goals. To be happy in a relationship, for example, you might choose orange juice for devotion. Pineapple juice, on the other hand, will manifest the happiness that comes from feeling welcome wherever you go. By the way, if you're a corned-beef-and-cabbage fan, there's no reason not to cook up some cabbage with the beef—this represents luck!

# Sunny-Side Salad

## (SERVES 3)

T ake a walk on the sunny side of the street with this healthy and joy-producing salad. Better still, if you've had trouble sleeping because of your mood, lore tells us that lettuce will calm your mind and give you a restful night.

**PREPARING YOUR CAULDRON** This salad should be prepared in a sunny location for best results. Take your components to a window that's receiving natural light (if the sun is shining, the results will improve dramatically). Let the ingredients sit there for a few moments and absorb all the warmth and blessings of the sun as you visualize your goal (if you have trouble coming up with an image, use the infamous happy face—it might be a cliché, but it has a strong sympathetic effect). When the exterior of the lettuce has gotten just slightly warm, it is then energized for your spell-recipe.

**COMPONENTS** * 1/4 head of radicchio lettuce * 1/2 head of Bibb lettuce * 1/4 head any other favorite lettuce * 1/2 cup thinly sliced scallions * 1/2 cup sliced green olives * 2 Tbsp. red wine vinegar * 1/3 cup olive oil * 1/2 tsp. *each* garlic and onion powder

**DIRECTIONS** Gently tear the lettuce (cutting it cuts off the magick) and put it in a large bowl with the scallions and olives. In another small container whisk the vinegar, oil, powders, salt, and pepper until well blended. Toss with the lettuce, visualizing your mood lifting just like the salad! This is an excellent opportunity to add an incantation like:

*Worries and sadness take to flight,*
*My mood will lift with every bite!*

**ENCHANTING ALTERNATIVES** Salads offer a lot of options for personal innovation. If you want to feel happy about what you have, add croutons (providence). For joy in more intuitive matters, go with a lunar addition like sliced cucumbers, which look like full moons, and for delight in a relationship add tomatoes, the "love apple"!

# Follow-Your-Bliss Barley Soup

## (SERVES 5)

This is great comfort food, making everyone who eats it feel warm, happy, and cozy. It's interesting to note that barley was often included in Indian wedding rites because of its joy-conferring quality and associations with fertility.

**PREPARING YOUR CAULDRON** It's hard to follow your bliss if you don't know for sure where it lies. Take the time to meditate for a few minutes each day for several days before preparing this spell-recipe. Think about the things that make you truly happy (and recognize the things that do not). This will help you better direct the energy of the spell-recipe.

**COMPONENTS** * 2 Tbsp. butter * 1 cup chopped red onions * ¹/₂ cup cauliflower florets * ¹/₂ cup broccoli florets * ¹/₂ cup chopped peeled potatoes * ¹/₂ cup chopped celery * ¹/₂ cup diced carrots * 5 cups beef stock * 5 cups chicken stock * 2 cups pearl barley * 1 ¹/₂ Tbsp. chopped fresh thyme * 1 ¹/₂ Tbsp. chopped fresh oregano * pinch of marjoram

**DIRECTIONS** Melt butter in a large soup pot (this melts away the barriers between you and true happiness). Add the vegetables and sauté lightly for 15 minutes over medium-low heat. Add the remaining ingredients and cook for 30–45 minutes until the barley is tender. As it cooks, focus on your goal, close your eyes (this improves focus for many people), and say:

*Barley sealed with magick's kiss, Renew in me a sense of bliss.*
*Joy to my mind, joy to my heart, Here, I claim, the magick impart!*

Serve with crusty bread and a tossed salad for a truly bliss-filled meal.

**ENCHANTING ALTERNATIVES** For truly sweet joy, add sweet potatoes. For happiness that has rich foundations in which to grow, add more root vegetables. Nonvegetarians can add some finely diced beef too, which will magickally manifest some good financial news that brings a lot of happiness with its timely arrival.

# Sassy Saffron Soup

## (SERVES 2)

B
U
B
B
L
E,

B
U
B
B
L
E,

T
O
I
L

&

T
R
O
U
B
L
E

**H**appiness has many dimensions, including a playful, mischievous one. So when you'd like a little sassy, bold jubilation, make this soup and watch your whimsical nature awaken. Saffron has long been considered an excellent spice to help with this goal, especially in the area of spiritual joy.

**PREPARING YOUR CAULDRON** In a swatch of soft cloth approximately 3 by 3 inches square place a small feather and a pinch of saffron. Focus on your goal, saying:

> *Magick to hold, for a personality* bold
> *Filled with humor and cheer, a little sassiness* here!

Tie up the bundle with a thread or piece of yarn and keep it with you both while enacting the spell-recipe and afterward as a portable charm that inspires sassy, silly, unbridled joy.

**COMPONENTS** * 2 Tbsp. olive oil * 1 cup trimmed Russian rye bread cubes * 2 large garlic cloves, minced * ¼ cup dry cooking wine * 2 cups canned low-salt chicken broth * 1 pinch of saffron threads * salt, to taste

**DIRECTIONS** In a skillet sauté the garlic for 2–3 minutes in the oil. Add the bread cubes, continuing to stir regularly until the bread is golden on all sides (note that the square shape of the cubes provides solid foundations on which your magick will grow). Add the remaining ingredients and bring to a low rolling boil (as bubbly as you want to be after eating it!). Lower heat and simmer for 30 minutes. The soup may be consumed as it is but is even better pureed, so you can whip up some extra positive energy before serving.

**ENCHANTING ALTERNATIVES** This soup is quite tasty topped with melted cheese, which adds love (especially self-love) into the magickal equation. You could also change the type of bread cubes to alter the focus. For example, use sourdough bread when you've been feeling particularly sour and want to transform that attitude.

# Serenity Sun Apples

## (MAKES 36 COOKIES)

W hen wanderlust or the seven-year itch begins to take hold, or you find that everything annoys you, make these cookies and redis-cover contentment with life just as it is. In Persia apricots are called sun apples, which may be why they became associated with joy. The shining of the sun on special occasions is considered a sign of divine favor.

**PREPARING YOUR CAULDRON** What area of your life needs a little more peace or joy? Etch a symbol of this into the bottom of the shells (e.g., a heart for contentment in a relationship). Also, before making this dish take a few minutes to meditate. Still your mind and spirit so that you don't take anx-iety into the kitchen—that won't produce contentment in the least! During your meditation, visualize bright white light filling every cell of your body, collecting any lingering negativity, and transporting it away.

**COMPONENTS** * ³/₄ cup dried apricots * 1 cup water * ¹/₄ cup brown sugar * 2 Tbsp. apple brandy * 2 Tbsp. powdered sugar * ¹/₂ cup heavy cream * 36 shortbread shells (or other pastry shell of choice)

**DIRECTIONS** Simmer the apricots, sugar, and water for 15 minutes until tender (this also tenderizes an apathetic or hardened heart). Transfer to a blender or food processor and puree completely. Set aside. Whip the heavy cream to gentle-peak stage. Fold in the brandy and sugar, saying:

*Happiness to me, contentment to me,*
*The magick's stirred, so mote it be!*

Fill pastry shells with alternating layers of cream and apricot puree. Chill for 30 minutes before serving.

**ENCHANTING ALTERNATIVES** You can use any fruit as the puree for this spell-recipe (if using fresh fruit, use 1 lb. fruit and reduce water to $1/4$ cup) and simply change the type of brandy you add to complement the flavors. How about raspberries and berry brandy for abundant joy, oranges and orange brandy for a happy relationship, or pears with pear brandy for long-lasting joy?

# CHAPTER 10

# MONEY MUNCHIES

**M**y mother was a wise, wonderful, and frequently witty woman. Although she knew money didn't buy happiness, it was her opinion that it sure made being happy a lot easier! I happen to agree.

Some of the ingredients commonly used to foster improved cash flow include:

ALFALFA * ALLSPICE * ALMONDS * BANANAS * BARLEY * BASIL *
BEANS * BERRIES * CABBAGE * CASHEWS * CHAMOMILE *
CHOCOLATE * CINNAMON * CLOVES * DILL * EGGS * FIGS *
GINGER * GRAPES * LETTUCE * MAPLE SYRUP * MARJORAM *
MILK * MINT * OATS * ONIONS * ORANGES * PARSLEY *
PEANUTS * PEARS * PEAS * PECANS * PINE NUTS * PINEAPPLE *
POMEGRANATES * RICE * SESAME SEEDS * SPINACH * TEA *
TOMATOES * WHEAT

Decorate your money buffet table with shades of green, silver, and gold. To this foundation, add a horn of plenty filled with grapes or berries and a vase overflowing with snapdragons and periwinkle. For crystals, jade is a good choice. Prepare these foods when the sun is high, and look to Anu (Celts), Jua P'ao (China), Fulla (Norway), or Njord (Scandinavian) as potential pantry protectors.

# Protect-Your-Prosperity
# Spinach Pasta
### (SERVES 2)

The wonderful green noodles in this spell-recipe represent your money, while the garlic sauce neatly surrounds it with protective energy. This way, when you really need money, you can bank on it being there!

**PREPARING YOUR CAULDRON** Make yourself a karmic piggy bank. To do this you'll need a plain bank (paintable, with a plug in the bottom), some black and white paint, and a special "seed coin" (perhaps a silver quarter or a coin that bears your birth year on it).

On the side of the bank paint a yin-yang symbol, which represents equitable balance in all things (including your money). After the paint dries, hold the seed coin over the opening of the bank, saying:

*What I place herein, multiply and bless threefold,*
*To others in charity, and to myself to hold.*

Drop the seed coin in the bank, and do the same with your loose change every day. When the bank is filled, give the proceeds except the seed coin to a good charity; the seed coin remains in the bank to bring the blessings back to you.

**COMPONENTS** * ¹/₂ lb. spinach noodles * 3 cloves garlic * 3 Tbsp. olive oil * ¹/₂ cup fresh chopped spinach * ¹/₂ cup grated Asiago or fresh Parmesan cheese

**DIRECTIONS** Bring a large pot of water to a full rolling boil and add the spinach noodles (both the color and the leafy nature of spinach encourage a flow of money). While these cook to a tender stage, sauté the garlic and chopped spinach in the olive oil. Drain the noodles and add the garlic blend, tossing gently, focusing on your goal, until well coated. This is an ideal time to add an incantation like:

*Oodles of noodles, with prosperity green*
*Bring me more money than I've ever seen!*

Serve with asiago cheese sprinkled liberally on top in the pattern of a dollar sign. Eat, and watch with joy as cash stays where it belongs—in your pocket and the bank!

**ENCHANTING ALTERNATIVES** For more protective energy, sauté 2 Tbsp. diced onion with the garlic. For more prosperity, dice up precooked broccoli spears and blend them in with the noodles and garlic.

# Cash-in-a-Flash Custard

## (YIELDS 3 CUPS)

The eggs and cream in this spell-recipe attract money, while the sugar makes its receipt ever so sweet and timely! Add a little green or yellow food coloring (representing gold) to improve the symbolic value.

**PREPARING YOUR CAULDRON** When I think of needing money quick, I think of my ATM card. So take a moment before preparing this spell-recipe to bless that card. The goal is to be able to access money when you need it most! To accomplish this, wait until the moon is full (for similar financial fullness) and hold the card in both hands, saying:

*Cash come quick, magick here bind,*
*When I need money, prosperity's mine!*

Repeat the incantation mentally each time you use the card to increase the overall effect.

**COMPONENTS** * 2 eggs * 2 egg yolks * 2 cups of light cream * ½ cup sugar * 1 vanilla bean * crushed nuts (optional garnish)

**DIRECTIONS** Combine the eggs, egg yolks, and sugar in a large bowl and beat them until they double in volume (5–7 minutes). This symbolically doubles the financial base with which you're working!

In a nonaluminum pan warm the light cream and vanilla bean together, but do *not* boil. Remove the vanilla bean and transfer the liquid to a double boiler. Add the egg mixture. Continue cooking in the top of the double boiler (over water) for 25 minutes or until the custard thickens. Remember to stir clockwise constantly and visualize money falling into the pan (think pennies from heaven with more oomph)! If you wish, you can repeat the previous incantation at this juncture too. Spoon out into dishes and chill.

**ENCHANTING ALTERNATIVES** Any of the herbs or fruits (in the form of an extract) mentioned at the beginning of this chapter could be added for variety or a slightly different focal point. For example, if you need extra physical energy to go out and seek your fortune, use ginger to flavor the custard.

# Currency Berry Crisp

## (SERVES 6–8)

There's nothing quite so nice as a crisp bill, which is why grandmothers everywhere give them as gifts. This spell-recipe builds on that tradition and symbolism.

**PREPARING YOUR CAULDRON** Building on the idea that one should give to receive, take a small bill (e.g., a five-dollar bill) and wrap it in paper three times, saying:

> *To one in need, this bill goes, There too, the money flows.*
> *And like a wave that moves to the sea, So prosperity returns to me!*

Put it in an envelope and mail it to someone anonymously, then prepare this spell-recipe.

**COMPONENTS** * 1 ½ lbs. frozen mixed berries * ¼ cup flour * 1 cup sugar * ¾ cup oats * ⅔ cup packed dark brown sugar * ½ tsp. ground ginger * ¼ tsp. ground nutmeg * 7 Tbsp. chilled unsalted butter, diced

**DIRECTIONS** Mix the berries with the sugar and flour and toss until coated. Place in a well-greased 9-inch pie pan and set aside. In another bowl blend the remaining ingredients together, cutting in the butter until it's well integrated. If this doesn't hold together when pinched, add a few drops of water until it does. Sprinkle evenly over the berries (move clockwise, and pattern the last bit like a dollar sign to manifest that cash quickly). Bake at 375 degrees for 1 hour.

Serve warm with a dollop of vanilla ice cream, which encourages insightful use of the cash that comes your way.

**ENCHANTING ALTERNATIVES** Add shaved almonds to either the berries or the topping for even greater prosperity power!

# Cents-and-Sensibility Apples

## (SERVES 3)

There are going to be times when everyone has to pinch pennies. This sweet dessert makes that process a little less painful and adds a hearty dose of wisdom, so you use your resources carefully.

**PREPARING YOUR CAULDRON** Use a variation on an old divination method to find out how long you will need to make resources last. Hold the first apple in the bunch in hand and count the number of turns it takes to twist out the stem. This number equals the number of days, weeks, or months.

**COMPONENTS** * ³/₄ lb. apples (your choice, but green emphasizes money) * 1 Tbsp. butter * 1 ¹/₂ Tbsp. maple syrup * ¹/₂ tsp. maple extract * ¹/₂ Tbsp. water * cinnamon and ginger, to taste

**DIRECTIONS** Peel the apples clockwise, taking care not to break the peels if possible. This encourages more luck with the food magick being created. Core them, then cut into ¹/₄-inch-thick slices. Save the peel and dry it for magickal incense.

Carve a dollar sign into each slice, then sauté the apple slices in butter until golden brown to energize the magick. Remember to keep your mind focused on your goal while you cook. Add the maple syrup and extract, water, and personally preferred spices (about a pinch is plenty). As this cooks it creates a natural glaze.

Serve warm to allay indifferent feelings that often arise with constraint. Or eat just before you try to rework your budget, so resources get applied in the best possible way.

**ENCHANTING ALTERNATIVES** Toss in some nuts to bring a little humor into the picture (humor is a great coping mechanism), and let yourself get a little "nutty"!

# Get-Rich-Quick Cabbage

## (SERVES 4 AS A SIDE DISH)

This dish originated in Germany, where it is consumed during the Christmas season to inspire abundance, especially in the area of good-will, kinship, and a sense of welcome. Better still, cabbage protects your abundance once it's obtained!

**PREPARING YOUR CAULDRON** Pour out a small cup of sangria or apple juice before you begin making the spell-recipe. Bless the cup by holding it in your strong hand (the one you write with), saying:

> *Minding dollars, minding cents, I cast this spell for abundance.*
> *Directed by will and by my inner witch, In all things I will become truly*
> *rich*

**COMPONENTS** * 1 small head of cabbage * 4 cups sangria or sweet red wine * 1 tsp. cinnamon * 1 tsp. salt * 2 Tbsp. butter * 2 tsp. sugar * 1 apple, grated

**DIRECTIONS** Slice the cabbage, thinking about eliminating any barriers between yourself and wealth as you slice. In a large bowl mix the cabbage with the wine, cinnamon, and salt and allow it to marinate in the refrigerator for at least 8 hours. Blend and mix it regularly (this is a good time to recite your incantation from the preparation process again). Drain, reserving the liquid.

Melt the butter in a skillet and add the drained cabbage. Brown gently, sprinkling sugar over the top to help caramelize the mix. Return the wine blend to the cabbage and simmer for 50 minutes. Add the apple and cook for 15 more minutes.

Think fond thoughts of family and friends as you eat this, and watch them return that fondness threefold.

**ENCHANTING ALTERNATIVES** Substitute carrots for the apple if you like. Steam the carrots to firm-tender stage and add during the last 15 minutes of cooking as with the apple.

# CHAPTER 11

# POT OF PROMISES

**P**romises, commitments, oaths, affidavits—our lives are filled with moments in which we are asked to guarantee ourselves on some level. In marriage we promise our hearts and devotion. At the signing of a loan, we promise to pay it back! But situations in life and our society don't always make it easy to keep our promises. So let's fill the kitchen cauldron with heaping quantities of tenacity, honest intention, and perseverance to help us keep our word and honor our pledges.

Some of the ingredients traditionally used for this purpose include:

BAY LEAVES * CUMIN * FIGS * GARLIC * HONEY * LEMONS *
LICORICE * MULBERRIES * NUTMEG * ONIONS * ORANGES *
PEANUT BUTTER * PLANTAINS * ROSE WATER * RYE * SALT *
SUNFLOWER SEEDS * TEA * WINE

The table for promise-keeping food should always be balanced, so that it reflects each person taking part in a commitment along with the commitment being made. Fill a centerpiece with magnolias for dedication, and set out a common cup from which all can drink to show agreement. Potential pantry protectors for promise keeping include Agashi and Inna (Nigeria), Chando (India), and Hebat (Hittites).

# Marriage Mead

## (YIELDS 4 CUPS)

**M**ead is a honey-based wine that was often used to seal promises, especially those given in love. Better still, according to Roman tradition, the honey in the mead will make your promises long lasting and incredibly eloquent and creative!

**PREPARING YOUR CAULDRON** When you're slicing the orange for this spell-recipe, get creative and shape the slices to look like hearts so they symbolize your intention. As you do, focus on the feelings you have in your heart and say:

> *Orange for fidelity, devotion,*
> *And true love abide with me!*

**COMPONENTS** * 1 liter dry red wine * 1 cup honey * ½ orange, peeled and sliced * 1 tsp. rose water

**DIRECTIONS** Using a nonaluminum pan, warm the wine gently on low (love should be gentle and warm, unless you're looking for passion—then you might consider a low rolling boil, but the flavor will be different). Add the sliced oranges, and then very slowly add the honey. The nice thing about honey is that it drizzles, so you can actually write with it on the top of the liquid. Scribe your name and that of your beloved or draw more hearts with the honey as you pour it. Taste the blend regularly and stop adding honey if it is becoming too sweet for you. Once the honey is thoroughly mixed in, add the rose water.

Serve warm to put a new spark into your commitment to a person or situation, or cold if you need to look at your promises with a cool head. As you take the cup to your lips, whisper your promise into the mead three times so you can honor it in body, mind, and spirit. Drink with pure motivations.

**ENCHANTING ALTERNATIVES** Add a bay leaf to improve your inner fortitude for promise keeping, and nutmeg for loyalty.

# Sweet-Potato Promises

## (SERVES 2 AS A SIDE DISH)

Potatoes tend to grow well in a variety of conditions, including harsh ones. Magickally, this symbolizes developing a lot of staying power to keep our promises no matter how difficult the circumstances appear!

**PREPARING YOUR CAULDRON** Set up the eating area to reflect the goal, which is improving the health of a relationship. Decorate with a red candle (love), and two white candles. Each person should light one white candle and whisper wishes for the relationship into the flame. Light the central candle together from the other two just before consuming this dish to symbolize your unity of heart and spirit.

**COMPONENTS** * 2 medium-sized sweet potatoes * 1 ½ Tbsp. olive oil * ½ tsp. ground cumin * ¼ cup minced scallion

**DIRECTIONS** Peel and shred the sweet potatoes while focusing on your goal to get rid of anything that deters or divides your allegiance. In a skillet sauté the shredded potatoes, cumin, and scallions in the olive oil. Add an incantation to energize the blend like:

> *Promises to make, promises to hold, Let our hearts be pure and our tongues be bold!*
> *A promise kept true, by this spell it's done, By our will, the magick's begun!*

Stir until cooked through (4–5 minutes).

**ENCHANTING ALTERNATIVES** Use red potatoes for commitments having to do with love, purple potatoes for spiritual commitments, and new potatoes for dedication to new projects.

# Security Salad

## (SERVES 4–6)

D evotion implies safety, security, and longevity. Lemons and onions support this goal by providing preservative power and protection.

**PREPARING YOUR CAULDRON** Consider the focus of your spell-recipe, the types of onions used in this dish, for example, for a variety of kinds of energy. For example, use white onions to manifest pure intentions, Spanish onions if you want your commitments to endure, and cooking onions for commitments having to do with domestic matters.

**COMPONENTS** * 3 cups thinly sliced red onions * $1/2$ cup parsley leaves * 2 Tbsp. olive oil * 1 lemon * 1 large garlic clove, minced * $1/4$ tsp. ground coriander * salt, to taste

**DIRECTIONS** Take care in slicing the onions so you get unbroken rings, which will help increase the protective power of this dish by surrounding the energy with a sacred circle. Rinse the onions gently, then drain. Place in a bowl with the remaining ingredients and chill for 30 minutes before serving. This will provide you with a clearer mind for whatever promise needs your attention. Just before serving, add an incantation like:

*Within these sacred circles, drawn round, My commitment shall abound.*
*Then when accepted, from without to within, So the magick shall begin.*

**ENCHANTING ALTERNATIVES** Toss in some sliced green olives if you would like to feel at peace with a promise regarding money, or black olives for a promise relating to personal health and well-being.

# Pledge Plantains

## (SERVES 2)

**P**lantains are an ideal promissory food, having often been used in wedding rituals to represent devotion. Many wise people are said to have enjoyed this vegetable-like fruit, which symbolically provides us with extra wisdom for making and executing our promises.

**PREPARING YOUR CAULDRON** Think of a symbol that represents your goal and carve this into each plantain slice after you've peeled and cut them. Focus wholly on your goal as you etch the emblem, so that the energy of that symbol cooks up with the rest of the spell-recipe.

**COMPONENTS** * 2 very ripe plantains * 4 Tbsp. unsalted butter * 2 Tbsp. rum * 1/2 cup coconut milk * 1 cup sugar * 1/4 cup heavy cream * 1/4 cup fresh ground coconut

**DIRECTIONS** Peel the plantains and slice them into 1/2-inch-thick slices (etch symbols at this juncture). Using a nonstick skillet, warm the butter on low until melted. Add the sliced plantains, coating thoroughly. Cook until the plantain slices are browned on each side. Remove from the pan with a slotted spoon and drain on paper towels.

To the remaining butter add the sugar and cook until caramelized. Blend the coconut milk with the rum and add to the sugar-butter mixture, whisking over low heat until fully blended. Since the whisk literally whips up some energy, this is a nice time to add a prayer like:

*Great spirit, I come to you,*
*Keep my commitments sure, my promises true!*

Add the plantains along with the cream, shaking the pan to mix the ingredients.

Serve topped with fresh coconut sprinkled in a circle around the outside of the plantains to protect your magic.

**ENCHANTING ALTERNATIVES** Add ½ tsp. of banana extract to improve the devotional energy in this dessert, ½ tsp. of vanilla extract if it's aimed at a loving relationship, and/or ½ tsp. of rum extract to safeguard a promise.

# Devotion-with-a-Twist Breadsticks

## (YIELDS 16 LARGE BREADSTICKS)

These breadsticks bind your magickal desire and your promise into the dough as you twist them into shape. Then eating them releases the magick to where you need it most—within!

**PREPARING YOUR CAULDRON** Make yourself a portable charm for commitment based on the idea for this spell-recipe. In Arabia and other parts of the world, knots were often used to bind energy and keep it safe until needed. In this case, tie some yarn or a small piece of sturdy cord into three knots, repeating this incantation thrice with each knot:

> *It is not the cord I bind, but my magick spell, Heed my words and heed them well.*
> *Commitment and devotion shall be found, When this knot is then unbound!*

Carry this with you anywhere you wish, untying a knot when you really need the energy. But never undo the third one. It should remain in place so you can reuse and recharge the charm.

**COMPONENTS** * 1 1-lb. loaf frozen bread dough * 2 Tbsp. aniseed, crushed * 1 Tbsp. fennel seeds, crushed * 2 Tbsp. powdered grated orange peel * cornmeal * 1 beaten egg * coarse salt (optional)

**DIRECTIONS** Defrost the bread dough according to package directions. Once it's completely defrosted, cover the dough with a cloth and let it rise for 30 minutes in a warm area. Knead the aniseed, fennel seed, and orange peel evenly into the dough, and then let it rise again for 1 hour. Remember that this process also "raises energy"!

Divide the dough into sixteen equal portions. Sprinkle the cornmeal on a large nonstick surface like a cookie sheet. On a flat surface, roll each of the dough pieces into a rope about 8 inches long, then roll the rope in the cornmeal. Twist into any magickal shape you need: try a heart for love or an equidistant cross representing balance and symmetry. With the cross shape you can add a verbal component by touching each of the four quarter points as you say:

*I affirm my words will be true to my promise [east],*
*I affirm giving ongoing energy to my promise [south],*
*I affirm my heart's desire to keep this promise [west],*
*I affirm my dedication to manifesting this promise [north].*

Place the twisted shapes on baking sheets to rise again for 45 minutes.

Preheat oven to 375 degrees. Brush the top of the bread twists with a little beaten egg, then sprinkle with salt. Bake for approximately 20 minutes until golden brown (they will sound hollow in the center if tapped lightly). Cool and enjoy!

**ENCHANTING ALTERNATIVES** If several people are involved in a promise, have each one roll out a rope and then weave the ropes into a braid. Eating the braid then indicates each person's acceptance of the promise made and his or her commitment to keeping it.

CHAPTER 12

# Psychic Platters

To be fully aware means awakening ourselves to all of the wonders and gifts that already exist in our spirits. Of these gifts, one of the most powerful for day-to-day magickal living is that of being psychically attuned. Our intuitive nature can help us avoid a lot of life's bumps and bruises. It also opens us to having a natural empathy with people, and thereby improves all our interactions.

Unlike in typical depictions, being psychic doesn't just mean being able to see into the future. "Psychic" comes from a root word that translates as "pertaining to the soul." In this context, psychism means listening to your dreams. It means bringing spirituality into your nine-to-five world, and it means releasing your special form of magick into the kitchen cauldron!

Here are the ingredients suited to this task:

BAMBOO SHOOTS * BAY LEAVES * BEAN SPROUTS (ALL) *
CARROTS * CAULIFLOWER * CELERY * CELERY SEED *
CINNAMON * CITRON * COCONUT * CUCUMBERS * DILL * FISH *
FLOWERS (GARNISH) * GRAPES * LEMONS * LETTUCE * MACE *
MINT * MUSHROOMS * NUTMEG * ONIONS * POTATOES *
ROSE WATER * THYME * TOFU * VEGETARIAN FARE

BUBBLE, BUBBLE, TOIL & TROUBLE

Decorate the dining area for psychic platters with those items you commonly use for personal spiritual endeavors (like tarot cards or candles). Consider having a centerpiece of honeysuckle, marigold, and rose accented with lapis stones to improve the overall ambiance and heighten your intuitive nature.

Generally psychic matters are ruled by the moon, so the phase from the waxing to the full moon is best for timing. Finally, call on Enki (Sumeria), Heka (Egypt), Locana (Tibet), or Minona (Dahomey) as pantry protectors.

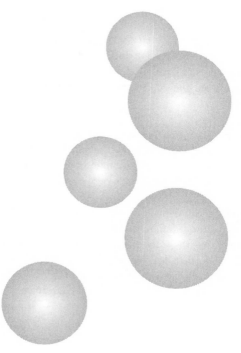

# Gypsy-Seer Soup

## (SERVES 6 AS AN APPETIZER)

All of the ingredients placed into this soup pot open your third eye wide to the spiritual energies around you every day. The slow cooking brings the ingredients' energies into harmony so you can accept new awareness at a pace that's wholly right for you.

**PREPARING YOUR CAULDRON** There's no reason not to have a little fun with this project, so why not dress for the role? Toss on a gypsy-style bandanna, pull out your crystal ball and use it as a decoration in your kitchen, and play lively music that lifts the energy and helps to move it where you want it to go.

**COMPONENTS** * 1 lb. orange roughy fillets * 2 Tbsp. lemon juice * chives, to taste * 2 onions, diced * 2 stalks celery, chopped * 1–2 Tbsp. butter * 1 8-oz. block tofu, cubed * 1 cup fresh mushrooms, sliced * 4 cups chicken stock * $1/2$ tsp. *each* salt, basil, and celery seed

**DIRECTIONS** Slice the orange roughy into 1-inch pieces. Rinse gently under cold water, then sprinkle with lemon juice to purify the energy. Meanwhile, sauté the chives, onions, and celery in the butter until tender. Add the tofu, mushrooms, stock, and seasonings. Bring to a low rolling boil and simmer for 20 minutes. Finally add the fish, simmering for 10 minutes until the fish is cooked, stirring clockwise, saying:

*I claim the power around me, I claim the power within me.*
*Open my senses and my inner sight, Raise my awareness to new heights!*

Serve in white bowls (representing the moon) and eat with an open mind! Afterward, why not try practicing with that crystal ball you brought into the sacred space at the outset? Make sure to take note of the results!

**ENCHANTING ALTERNATIVES** To keep your visionary sense clear of pre-conceived notions, add purifying herbs or vegetables to this blend (like garlic or other varieties of onions).

# Full-Moon Magick Pies

## (YIELDS 13 PIES)

The moon is among the most powerful symbols used repeatedly in magickal traditions. This spell-recipe helps you internalize all that symbolic power and awareness. In China, people prepare these little treats during the moon festival that takes place in the middle of the eighth lunar month, which is also thought to be the moon's birthday.

**PREPARING YOUR CAULDRON** I strongly suggest waiting for a full moon to create this spell-recipe, as the timing greatly empowers your magick. Dress in silver or white (which honors the moon) and leave an offering to the moon on your rooftop, saying:

> *Lady Moon with silvery light,*
> *Hear my wishes on this night*
> *And bring to me inner sight.*

**COMPONENTS** * 1 package piecrust mix * ½ cup chopped dates * 1 cup diced dried apricots * 1 cup shredded sweetened coconut * 1 cup raisins * 1 cup finely chopped walnuts * ¼ cup grated lemon rind (optional) * ¼ cup sugar

**DIRECTIONS** Prepare the piecrust according to package directions. Roll it out into a large square or rectangle and cut into twenty-six 1-inch triangles. Into each of the triangles carve the image of an eye using a toothpick to represent "vision."

136

Blend the fruits and nuts together and divide the mixture up evenly on thirteen of the triangles, one for each moon of the year. Dampen the edges of the bottom triangle and lay another triangle on top, pinching the sides together firmly. Bend the edges of the little pies so they're slightly curved to look like the moon. Sprinkle a mixture of lemon rind and sugar on top, then bake in a 375-degree oven for about 25 minutes until golden brown. Let the pies sit in lunar light to charge them up thoroughly before eating.

**ENCHANTING ALTERNATIVES** Add a little vanilla extract to the fruit mixture to bring "perfect love" (and/or good intentions) into all your psychic endeavors.

# Fortune-telling Fish

## (SERVES 4)

B
U
B
B
L
E,

B
U
B
B
L
E,

T
O
I
L

&

T
R
O
U
B
L
E

**A**ncient tales are swimming with magickal fish. Ra was guided through the underworld by fish, Chinese lore uses fish as an emblem of freedom, and in Victorian America fish was eaten to inspire prophetic dreams! All this makes a pretty strong foundation for using fish as part of our divinatory and spiritual diets.

**PREPARING YOUR CAULDRON** Consider the area of your life to which you need to apply a little more mystical insight and adjust the fish in this spell-recipe accordingly. For example, the snapper might be excellent for those conversations in which you'd like to be a little ahead of the game and ready with a snappy comeback! White fish of any sort has lunar overtones, and shellfish implies protecting yourself from unwanted psychic input.

**COMPONENTS** * 3–4 dried mushrooms * 1 1/2 lbs. red snapper fillets * 1 tsp. salt * 2 slices bacon * 1 8-oz. can bamboo shoots * 2 scallions, diced * 3 slices fresh ginger, minced * 1 Tbsp. sherry

**DIRECTIONS** Soak the mushrooms for 30 minutes until softened, then finely dice. Cook bacon, drain, and crumble. Mix the bacon with the bamboo shoots, scallions, ginger, mushrooms, and sherry. Make tiny cuts along the fish to allow flavoring to get inside. Salt the fish lightly and put it onto a heat-safe plate that will fit into a steamer. Pour the mushroom blend over the fish, saying:

*Steamy fortunes rising thick, Tell me true and tell me quick,*
*What will happen by 'n' by? Tell me where my future lies!*

Steam for 15 minutes until the fillets are flaky. Eat just prior to using your favorite divination tool.

**ENCHANTING ALTERNATIVES** There are certainly many varieties of mushrooms and herbs that could be substituted into this dish. Determine the area of your life on which you want to focus for a forthcoming divination effort. For example, a hint of rose water in the blend would aid in love or relationship questions, whereas garlic (protective energy) might help you uncover the cause of a magickal or psychic attack.

# Transcendental Tofu Burgers

## (SERVES 4)

O ne of the ultimate goals of kitchen magick is to transcend ho-hum dishes, transforming them into magickal menus. In this spell-recipe we're using a blend of vegetarian delights to purify the spirit and open the pathway for visions.

**PREPARING YOUR CAULDRON** Use this as an opportunity to take proper care of your personal divination tools. Pull out your runes, tarot cards, or crystal ball and cleanse them by passing them through a purgative incense like myrrh. Afterward, recharge the set by placing each in the light of the sun (for mental keenness) and the moon (for the intuitive nature). Finally, find a special housing for your tools so they won't be tampered with by unwanted hands or paws when not in use. Keep these items with you in the sacred kitchen while you prepare this spell-recipe to improve its connection with your personal energy and bless it with the magick you're creating.

**COMPONENTS** * 1 12-oz. package firm tofu * ¹/₂ cup grated carrot * ¹/₂ cup grated green onions * 2 tsp. minced ginger * 1 garlic clove, minced * ¹/₂ cup almonds, finely chopped * 1 large egg, beaten * 4 tsp. soy sauce * tomato slices and alfalfa sprouts (garnish)

**DIRECTIONS** Use a food grinder or food processor to grate the tofu into very fine granules and drain completely (this may require allowing the tofu to sit on paper towels for about 1 hour). The magickal benefit here is twofold: breaking down the barriers that you may have within to truly accepting your magickal gifts, and draining away any unwanted energies that the food may have picked up at the supermarket.

Blend the drained tofu with the remaining ingredients as you might to make a meat loaf. Add bread crumbs and/or water as needed to get a good consistency. Divide into fourths and shape each into a hearty-sized tofu burger (four is also the number that puts foundations under your visions). Grill these on low for about 15 minutes, then on medium heat for about 3 more minutes on each side until golden brown. Note that you can add any favorite sauce during the last turn along with an incantation like:

> *Renew my spirit, let me trust in my gifts. Remove the veil, all doubts lift.*
> *Psychic talents are a heritage true, In me awakened again, by this*
> *    magickal brew.*

Serve on fresh buns with sliced tomatoes and sprouts so your magickal insights likewise sprout to the forefront.

**ENCHANTING ALTERNATIVES** The beauty of this burger is that you can substitute many different vegetables in place of carrots simply by changing the spices slightly. Eliminate the ginger and use chopped broccoli, for example. This new blend will protect you from any unwanted influences during divinatory or psychic endeavors, whereas adding spinach improves your insight with questions pertaining to personal resources (both physical and financial).

# CHAPTER 13

# RELATIONSHIP REFRESHMENTS

Have you heard the phrase "No man is an island"? These days it's more true than ever. Passing acquaintances at the office, close friends, lovers, life mates, parents, children—all these people connect with us, and often change us in dramatic ways. That's one of the reasons relationship spell-recipes are so important. As we accept the energy in them, we also prepare ourselves to give and receive love: the most powerful magick of all.

Here are some of the ingredients that wise people throughout history have used to help star-crossed lovers or heal broken hearts:

APPLES * BARLEY * BASIL * BAY LEAVES * CABBAGE * CATNIP *
CHEESE * CHERRIES * CHESTNUTS * CHOCOLATE * CINNAMON *
DILL * GINGER * HONEY * KIWIS * LEMONS * MARJORAM *
NUTMEG * ORANGES * PARSLEY * RASPBERRIES *
STRAWBERRIES * SUGAR * TOMATOES * VANILLA * WINE

Decorate the relationship table with turquoise stones and gentle colors. In relationships people shouldn't scream at one another, and neither should your presentation. As for flowers, roses of all colors are definitely in order. Pantry protectors for these dishes include Albina (Etruria), Ishtar (Babylonia), and Kama and Krishna (India).

# Sweetheart Brownies

## (YIELDS 20 BROWNIES)

Cook these delicious mate-attracting treats to sweeten your love life.

**PREPARING YOUR CAULDRON** Grab a handful of bread crumbs and take them to an east-facing window of your home or apartment. Hold them for a moment, thinking of all the best attributes you'd like in a partner. Finally, release them to the four winds, which will carry your wishes out to the world.

**COMPONENTS** * 1½ cups butter * 12 oz. semisweet chocolate chips * 6 large eggs * 1¼ cups flour * 1 cup unsweetened cocoa powder * 3 cups sugar * ½ tsp. salt

**DIRECTIONS** Oil and lightly flour a 9 x 13–inch pan. Don't forget to draw hearts in the oil with your finger! Melt the butter and chocolate together in a saucepan. When the butter and chocolate are fully melted and blended, whisk in the eggs one at a time, followed by the dry ingredients, saying:

*Loving glances, sweet romances*
*Through this wonderful treat, my true love to meet!*

Bake at 350 degrees for 45 minutes.

Cool and enjoy! Sprinkle a little powdered sugar on top to make your new relationship all the more sweet.

**ENCHANTING ALTERNATIVES** Use white chocolate for a blond partner, mint extract for a wealthy mate or one with green eyes, or butterscotch flavoring for a red-headed mate.

# Caveat Crab

## (SERVES 3)

**E**very once in a while there's a person who seems wholly inaccessible and unapproachable, even as a friend. When this happens, and you'd like some magick to open the door and put that individual on "notice" that you're interested, this is a good spell-recipe to help break down the barriers.

**PREPARING YOUR CAULDRON** This spell-recipe is designed only to make the desired person aware of your interest, *not* manipulate his or her interest in you. Consequently, it's important to preface this spell-recipe with a prayer that allows the universe (or your pantry protector) to use your energy in the best possible way. One example directed to Kama would be:

> *Kama, god of love, born from Brahma's heart, See my desire, hear my wish. Let _____ [name] know my feelings, But be not constrained by them, For the greatest good, And it harm none. So be it.*

**COMPONENTS** * 1 ½ lbs. crabmeat * 2 Tbsp. butter * 1 Tbsp. olive oil * 1 16-oz. can spinach * 2 cups grape tomatoes * ½ cup yellow tomato, diced * 1 shallot, minced * 1 tsp. basil * ⅓ cup olive oil * ¼ cup balsamic or white wine vinegar * 1 tsp. fresh lemon juice * salt and pepper, to taste

**DIRECTIONS** Sauté the crabmeat in a combination of olive oil and butter. Drain on paper towels and set aside, keeping the meat warm. Lay out the spinach, drained, in a lightly oiled ovenproof pan (feel free to pattern it symbolically if time allows). Place the crabmeat evenly over the spinach. In a separate container mix all the remaining ingredients to create a dressing, and spoon evenly over top of the crabmeat. Warm in a 350-degree oven for about 10–15 minutes (to generate energy and warm hearts), saying:

*Let barriers melt away in the heat,*
*Let eyes see true the intention of my heart.*
*Interest be known; goodwill impart.*

Serve. Watch for opportunities to present themselves within the next few days.

**ENCHANTING ALTERNATIVES** If you're not sure that your intentions are wholly honorable in this situation, add a little onion and garlic to the sauce to purify those motivations. The dressing is also quite tasty on chicken or salads, both of which emphasize healthy relationships.

# Splitsville Splits

## (SERVES 1)

This wonderful no-guilt dessert is perfect when you want to get out of a relationship, when you'd like an overamorous lover to cool off for a while, or when you need to improve your spirits after a nasty split-up.

**PREPARING YOUR CAULDRON** If this spell-recipe is directed at cooling off a lover, take his or her picture and freeze it in an ice tray before starting the spell. This literally puts his or her attentions "on ice."

If you need to prepare for a split-up or heal a broken heart, cut out a piece of red paper in the shape of a heart and apply some salve to it. Fold this in on itself three times, saying:

*Peace of mind, peace of soul,*
*Peace of heart, make me whole.*

Carry this charm with you when cooking and thereafter until the situation has worked itself out.

**COMPONENTS** * ⅓ cup diced strawberries * 2 Tbsp. coconut-flavored rum * 1 banana, peeled and halved lengthwise * 1 cup raspberry sherbet or frozen yogurt * 1 cup coconut sherbet (or other favorite flavor) * 1 Tbsp. shredded sweetened coconut (garnish)

**DIRECTIONS** Marinate the strawberries overnight, refrigerated, in the rum. This purifies the energies in the berries so only pure feelings, without guilt or remorse, remain. Place the banana halves in a large bowl and top with sherbet or yogurt. Garnish with strawberries and a sprinkling of coconut.

Eat slowly, letting the sherbet melt in your mouth even as you want your sadness or misgivings to melt away!

**ENCHANTING ALTERNATIVES** For greater healing power, top with whipped cream. Cream symbolizes the mother aspect of the goddess, who is always there when we need comforting.

# Safe-Haven Salad

## (SERVES 4)

Everyone deserves at least one relationship in their lives in which they feel completely safe and secure. This spell-recipe helps bring such a relationship your way or foster one that already exists, and is particularly suited to a family to inspire greater unity and trust.

**PREPARING YOUR CAULDRON** You will need a pouch, box, or other small storage container that you can leave somewhere undisturbed for this spell. You will also need a picture of the individuals you wish to safeguard. Place the picture(s) in the container, saying:

*Protection within, this spell begins,*
*With magick pure, keep our family secure.*

Close the container and wrap it with a white ribbon or piece of yarn so the top doesn't come off accidentally. Keep this near your stove somewhere safe (this is the heart of the home). Here it will absorb all the good energy from your kitchen magick.

**COMPONENTS** * ½ cup pearl barley, presoaked * 1 ½ cups canned broth (your choice) * 1 large green pepper, diced * 1 small red bell pepper, diced * 2 large plum tomatoes, seeded and chopped (about 1 cup) * 1 cup fresh corn kernels * ¼ cup chopped green onions * 2 ½ Tbsp. orange juice * 2 Tbsp. olive oil * salt and pepper, to taste

**DIRECTIONS** Place the barley in a pan with your chosen broth over medium heat. Bring to a boil and simmer until the barley absorbs most of the broth (about 40 minutes). Mix the barley, peppers, tomatoes, corn, onion, juice, olive oil, salt, and pepper in a mixing bowl. The mixture coats the barley in protective energy. While you're mixing, add an incantation like:

> *Here place my magick, my will affect*
> *To preserve, love, and forever protect!*

Serve when warmed through for a warm, cozy relationship and home.

**ENCHANTING ALTERNATIVES** Substitute rice for the barley to produce a relationship that is both emotionally and financially secure.

RELATIONSHIP

REFRESHMENTS

149

# Cherish-Me Cheese Pasta
## (SERVES 4)

**C**heese was often part of wedding rituals in ancient times, in part because it was considered a gift from Apollo's son, Aristaeus. Aristaeus means "very good," and this spell-recipe is just that—very good tasting and very good for creating loving energy.

**PREPARING YOUR CAULDRON** To honor Apollo, open your kitchen curtains wide to receive sunlight and let that wonderful warmth bless your food and your efforts. Lighting a yellow or gold candle will also work if it happens to be a cloudy day.

**COMPONENTS** * 3 Tbsp. garlic, minced * ½ tsp. dried rosemary, crumbled * 1 Tbsp. butter * 1 Tbsp. olive oil * ¼ cup brandy * 1 cup heavy cream * ⅓ cup basket cheese, crumbled * ¾ cup cheese (your choice), crumbled * ½ cup freshly grated Parmesan and Romano mixed * ¾ lb. pasta (your choice)

**DIRECTIONS** Sauté the garlic and herbs in the butter and olive oil on low until golden brown and very aromatic (love tends to be strongly affected by aromas). Add the brandy and the cream slowly, stirring constantly and mixing well (cream has very nurturing energy). Add the cheese a little at a time, allow it to melt and mingle, and continue to simmer for 10 minutes after all the cheese has been added to integrate the flavors and the associated energy fully. Note that you will need to keep stirring to avoid separation or sticking (remember to turn your spoon clockwise to invoke the best possible energy).

While the sauce simmers, bring the pasta to a boil in a large pan. Cook until tender, drain, then put into a large bowl. Pour the sauce over the pasta, mixing until well coated. As you blend, add an incantation like:

*Love be quick, love be kind*
*Help me, Aristaeus, a lover find!*

**ENCHANTING ALTERNATIVES** Experiment with different types of cheese to attract specific kinds of lovers. For example, if you want a spicy lover, use a hot pepper cheese, or for a mature lover, use a well-aged cheese.

# CHAPTER 14

# SAFETY SUSTENANCE

From a spiritual vantage point, the distance between us and the stars is but a thought. Even so, that doesn't mean there aren't dangers in between and other precarious items that require our attention on a day-to-day level. From the negative energies created by over-population and stress to more mundane things like reckless drivers, people need protection on all levels of being.

As a child I remember my mother saying "safety first" and wondering what that meant. As an adult, I know. The idea behind safety sustenance is that of creating an aura of protection in and around yourself that goes with you everywhere, and even precedes you to clear the way of hazards.

Some of the ingredients used for protection include:

ALMONDS * ARTICHOKES * BANANAS * BASIL * BAY LEAVES *
BIRCH BEER * BROCCOLI * BRUSSELS SPROUTS * CAYENNE *
CHIVES * CLOVES * CORN * CRANBERRIES * DILL * EGGS *
GARLIC * HORSERADISH * JALAPENO PEPPERS * LEEKS *
MARJORAM * MUSTARD * NETTLE * OLIVE OIL * ONIONS *
PARSLEY * PEPPERS * PINEAPPLE * PRICKLY PEAR * RADISHES *
RASPBERRIES * RED RICE * RHUBARB * ROSEMARY * RUM *
SALSA * SESAME SEEDS * SUNFLOWER SEEDS * TOMATOES *
VINEGAR

To my way of thinking, protection is a very proactive and conscious thing. As the old saying goes, "Forewarned is forearmed." So prepare these dishes in daylight to accent the conscious self and its awareness of blatant and subtle dangers. Create a centerpiece using a cactus, or perhaps some carnation petals placed gently in a geode. For pantry protectors turn to Bes (Egypt), Perun (Slavonia), Inanna (Sumeria), and Artemis (Greece).

# Radical-Action Radishes

## (SERVES 6)

Folklore tells us that eating radishes keeps one safe from one's enemies, so this spell-recipe is ideal when you know you have adversaries and have to face them head-on. The red color and zesty flavor make this an ideal all-around protection food too.

**PREPARING YOUR CAULDRON** In keeping with the color theme, don something red (really *red*). This makes a very positive statement about your power in this situation. Red's vibration is also that of vibrant success, and according to folklore it scares away mischievous entities too!

**COMPONENTS** * 1 ½ lbs. red radishes * 1 tsp. salt * 2 tsp. sesame oil * 2 tsp. red wine vinegar * 4 tsp. soy sauce * 2 tsp. finely chopped onion (optional)

**DIRECTIONS** Trim the tops and bottoms of the radishes and rinse them thoroughly in cold water to cleanse any unwanted energy. Using the back of a spoon or knife, crush them slightly to crush any negativity aimed at you. Toss with salt and let stand at room temperature for 15 minutes. Blend in the remaining ingredients, mixing until the radishes are evenly coated, saying:

> *Within me power burns,*
> *All ill will, my magick turns!*

Chill before serving to help cool down an overheated situation.

**ENCHANTING ALTERNATIVES** Diced tomato and red pepper taste quite nice in this blend and add even more protective energy.

# Protective Pumpkin 'n' Squash

## (SERVES 3–4)

**P**umpkins appear most commonly around the Halloween holiday as a decorative or dessert item. In carved form they confer protection from any mischievous spirits, being a natural symbol of the golden sun. Squash was a staple in the New World, often safeguarding people from starvation.

**PREPARING YOUR CAULDRON** This is an ideal dish to prepare in the fall, so why not decorate accordingly? Buy an extra small pumpkin or squash and carve it like a jack-o'-lantern. Put a candle inside and light up your kitchen with watchful magick!

**COMPONENTS** * 1 5-lb. pumpkin * 1 tsp. butter * 2 stalks celery * 1 large Spanish onion, chopped * 2 tsp. fresh chopped garlic * 1 cup sliced mushrooms (your choice) * 2 cups cubed butternut squash * 1 Tbsp. ginger * $\frac{1}{2}$ cup bread crumbs * 1 egg * 1 Tbsp. brown sugar * 2 tsp. soy sauce

**DIRECTIONS** Cut off the top and clean out the pumpkin as you might for carving (symbolically this also cleans out any unwanted energy that's lingering around your home or life). Around the top rim, etch decorative magickal carvings like runes to accent your purpose. Lightly oil the outside of the pumpkin, put the top on, place it in a baking pan with a little water in the bottom, and bake at 350 degrees.

While the pumpkin begins to bake, sauté the celery, onion, and garlic in butter until lightly browned. To this add the mushrooms, squash, and ginger and cook for 10 minutes. Remove from the heat and toss with bread crumbs, egg, brown sugar, and soy sauce. Remove pumpkin from the oven and lift lid. Pour mixture into the pumpkin shell, replace lid, and bake for another 45 minutes until the pumpkin is soft, saying:

*Safety cooks from within, and this spell begins.*
*All evil abate, it's time to celebrate!*

When you serve, move your kitchen jack-o'-lantern to the dining area to support and ignite your magick.

**ENCHANTING ALTERNATIVES** To protect a relationship, add chopped almonds to the stuffing (about ¼ cup). To protect your mental well-being, use walnuts.

# Preservation Beets

## (SERVES 6 AS A SIDE DISH)

Having been associated with love goddesses in ancient Greek tradition and thereafter, beets are an ideal vegetable to safeguard those things and people you love during hard times. Additionally, this is a good dish to eat on Lammas to protect yourself from wicked fairies, who hate the color red!

PREPARING YOUR CAULDRON Bring into the sacred cooking space a picture of your loved ones or a representation of anyone or anything to which you want this magickal energy directed. Put those photos or items in your line of sight, so you can have a strong visual-emotional connection while you're working and focus the protective energy wholly on those individuals or items.

COMPONENTS * 3 lbs. fresh beets * $^2/_3$ cup sour cream * 2 Tbsp. horseradish * $^1/_2$ tsp. grated lemon or orange zest * 2 Tbsp. butter * 1 Tbsp. minced green onions

DIRECTIONS Wash and peel the beets. As you peel, imagine you are peeling away any barriers between the energy you're creating and the people to whom it's directed. Bake the beets at 350 degrees for 1 hour in a foil-covered baking dish with $^1/_4$ cup of water in the bottom. Pour any juice from the beets into a saucepan and set aside.

When the beets have cooled, cut into $^1/_4$-inch circular slices (the circle represents wholeness and completion) and return to the baking dish. In another bowl, blend the sour cream with the horseradish, beet juice (which provides lovely red color), and zest. Gently sauté the green onions in the butter and then add to the sour cream blend. Pour the mixture over the beet slices and rewarm. As you place this dish in the oven, add an incantation like:

*Within these beets are magick wards. Into each, my will is poured.*
*Keep my love safe, by this magick charm. My love protects and preserves*
*from all that would harm!*

**ENCHANTING ALTERNATIVES** Nestle the beets on a bed of cooked spinach for the strength to withstand any difficulties. Or eliminate the beets in this spell-recipe altogether and serve the sour cream sauce over cooked peas instead. Magickally, this "preserves the peas (peace)" in situations where you feel that anger and tension are causing peril.

# Sweet Sanctuary Sauce

## (YIELDS 2 ½ CUPS)

The word "sanctuary" implies a great sense of safety—of knowing that the place you are in and the people who surround you are wholly protected. This sauce provides that energy. You can eat it as a side dish or as a garnish for meat or ice cream.

**PREPARING YOUR CAULDRON** Since your home and kitchen are now a sacred space as a result of all the magick you're creating there, take a moment to bless this space or thank your pantry protectors for their aid. A simple prayer like this might do the trick:

> *Spirit of hearth and home, create here an atmosphere of safety and comfort. Surround this space with your protective power and bless it and the work of my hands with the light of love and joy. So be it.*

**COMPONENTS** * 1 12-oz. bag cranberries * 1 seedless orange, peeled * 1 10-oz. package frozen raspberries, thawed * ½ cup firmly packed light brown sugar (or to taste) * ¾ cup orange juice

**DIRECTIONS** Grind the cranberries and orange using a food processor or hand grinder. Symbolically this destroys any negativity. Place in a saucepan with the remaining ingredients. Simmer for 30 minutes on low, stirring regularly, until the sugar is completely dissolved and the blend thickens. Make sure to stir clockwise to attract more positive energy or counterclockwise to banish dangers while repeating an empowering phrase like:

*Surround, surround, protection abounds!*

Serve warm for active energy, or cold to cool down an overheated situation and inspire peace.

**ENCHANTING ALTERNATIVES** Pour this sauce neatly around pieces of poultry, symbolizing your desire to surround yourself with protection. Alternatively, substitute strawberries for the raspberries and add a hint of vanilla to protect a marriage from negativity and strengthen loving energies.

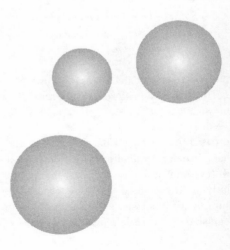

# Stand-Your-Ground Salsa

## (YIELDS 3 CUPS)

Sometimes the greatest protection comes in the form of self-confidence—an attitude that says "Don't even try it." This spicy salsa energizes that kind of demeanor, adding a little personal zest for good measure.

**PREPARING YOUR CAULDRON** The way others perceive your level of confidence has a lot to do with auric energies. Before making this spell-recipe, visualize pale red sparklers pouring down into your aura from above. These act like little balls of power and firm attitude spelled with a capital *A!* You will likely begin to feel a little warmer and more energized as the visualization takes effect. This is a good sign that you're doing it correctly. Allow some of these sparklers to pour out of your hands as you prepare the food.

**COMPONENTS** * 2 Tbsp. vegetable oil * $^1/_2$ lb. beefsteak tomatoes, peeled and chopped * 2 large yellow tomatoes, diced * 2 yellow peppers, chopped * 1 large onion, finely chopped * 1 jalapeno chili, minced * 1 celery stalk, minced * 1 small carrot, minced * $^1/_2$ cup red pepper, minced * $^1/_2$ cup red onion, minced * 2 Tbsp. lemon juice * $^1/_2$ tsp. salt

**DIRECTIONS** This is marvelously simple. Mix all of the ingredients together in a large food-storage container and store in the refrigerator, shaking regularly to integrate the flavors. The salsa is ready to be eaten in 2–3 hours, but tastes best if left overnight. Each time you shake, add an incantation like:

*Pepper, onions, spices fine, Within this mix protection shines.*
*Magick here with jalapeno minced, To fill me with self-confidence.*

Serve with tortilla chips and take a real bite out of your problems!

**ENCHANTING ALTERNATIVES** For even more flavor and safety, add 2 Tbsp. garlic juice or 1–2 Tbsp. minced garlic.

## CHAPTER 15

# SEXY SERVINGS

M any people would enjoy a little more spark and sizzle in their love lives. Whether simply awakening your own senses or creating an atmosphere filled with passionate expectation, sexy servings are a great help. The only caution I'd issue is that your partner should know about your kitchen cauldron's intentions. Otherwise the energy becomes manipulative, which spoils the mood totally!

Some of the ingredients traditionally used to motivate, arouse, kindle, and ignite desire include:

BEANS (MEN) * BLACKBERRIES * BRANDY * CARAWAY SEED *
CARDAMOM * CARROTS * CELERY * CHERRIES * CHOCOLATE *
CINNAMON * FIGS * FISH * GINGER * HONEY * MANGOES *
MINT * MUSTARD * NUTMEG * OLIVES * OYSTERS (WOMEN) *
PARSLEY * PEACHES * PLUM WINE * RASPBERRIES * RICE *
ROSE WATER * SESAME SEEDS * SHELLFISH * STRAWBERRIES *
TRUFFLES * VANILLA * YAMS

The meals in this chapter are best served by candlelight. Rather than worrying too much about your table, adorn yourself in a pleasing manner; women can add a dab of vanilla, lavender, jasmine, or cinnamon oil to their pulse points and men, clove, patchouli, vetiver, or musk. Tuck a carnelian stone in your pocket to maintain physical energy, then let nature take her course.

Pantry protectors for passionate meals include Aphrodite and Eros (Greece), Astarte (Phoenicia), and Jarilo (Slavic countries).

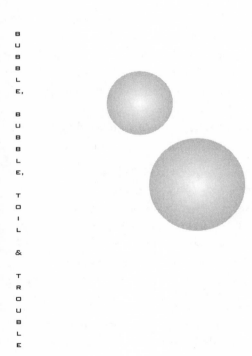

# Sassy Sizzling Shrimp

## (SERVES 2)

**E**ating shrimp, for me, is a sensual experience in itself! Our ancestors must have agreed, as they often ate shrimp to inspire passion and desire. If you're not fond of shrimp, any shellfish can be used in this provocative spell-recipe.

**PREPARING YOUR CAULDRON** Consider some of the physical or emotional characteristics of your lover and adapt the spell-recipe accordingly. For example, is he or she dark-haired? Use dark beer! A blond? There are blond beers on the market too! How about highly energetic? Sprinkle the batter with something a little spicy like cayenne or ginger. Note that if you're not already in a physical relationship, you can choose these ingredients according to the type of lover you most desire.

**COMPONENTS** * 2 eggs * 1 ⅓ cup flour * 1 tsp. salt * 2 tsp. sesame seeds * 1 cup flat beer or water * 1–1 ½ lbs. large shrimp * oil for deep frying

**DIRECTIONS** Start heating the oil in a deep pan or fryer. You will want enough so that the shrimp will not touch the bottom of the pan as they cook. Stir the eggs, flour, salt, sesame seeds, and beer together into a bowl with clockwise motions until the batter is smooth, saying:

> *Egg and magick in every bite, So too our passion shall ignite.*
> *Salt and beer and sesame, Give to us [me] our [my] fantasy!*

Dip the shrimp into the batter so that they are evenly coated and deep-fry until golden brown, so the shrimp become as "hot" as you wish your date to be!

Serve with cocktail sauce or a hearty portion of savory butter (mix 2 Tbsp. softened butter with 1 Tbsp. toasted sesame seeds, 1 tsp. Worcestershire sauce, and a hint of garlic). Eat creatively!

**ENCHANTING ALTERNATIVES** If you've never had fruited fish, it's an interesting taste sensation. Substitute plum wine for the beer for a slightly fruity flavor and serve with orange butter (butter mixed with orange juice and orange zest). The plum inspires healthy physical interest, while orange motivates devotion.

# Luscious Lusty Oysters

## (SERVES 2)

I know of no one who doesn't think of oysters when they think about aphrodisiacs. Better still, oysters naturally stimulate psychic awareness so we can anticipate our partners and please them even more!

**PREPARING YOUR CAULDRON** Use one of the oyster shells as an eros charm. Rinse it off in hot salt water, then situate any small oblong stone or object inside (this symbolizes sexual union). Tie the two halves of the shell together around the object with a red or purple ribbon (the color of passion), saying:

*Two minds, two hearts, two bodies, Connected in mutual pleasure, Protected by trust, And warmed with love.*

Keep this charm in the kitchen with you while you make this dish, and then perhaps leave it in the bedroom where it can effect the most good.

**COMPONENTS** * ¾ cup salad dressing * 1 green onion, minced * 2 Tbsp. dried cranberries, chopped * 2 Tbsp. orange juice * 5 Tbsp. yellow cornmeal * 2 Tbsp. flour * 1 lb. shucked large oysters, halved and drained well * 1 clove garlic, quartered * ¼ cup olive oil

**DIRECTIONS** Begin by mixing the salad dressing with onion, cranberries, and 1 Tbsp. orange juice. Set aside to use as a sauce. If you wish, you can repeat the incantation used for the charm at this point to empower the sauce with your magick and will.

In another shallow bowl mix the cornmeal, flour, and remaining orange juice. Coat the oysters with this mixture. Using a nonstick skillet, heat the olive oil and garlic together, removing the garlic when it smells aromatic. Turn the oysters into the heated oil, frying on each side for 2–3 minutes until browned.

Serve with a hearty portion of sauce drizzled over the top (don't be afraid to get creative with the pattern in which you apply the sauce)!

**ENCHANTING ALTERNATIVES** Lemon juice is a suitable substitute for orange juice, inspiring love and happiness in your physical encounters.

# Finger Lickin' Chicken

## (SERVES 4)

**W**hat is it that you most crave in your physical expressions? Tenderness? Joy? Playfulness? Intensity? No matter that craving or to whom it's directed, this dish creates the right auric energies to express that desire effectively to your partner.

**PREPARING YOUR CAULDRON** Expressing your desires is often a function of self-confidence. To help with this, take a long hot bath scented with heather (for attractiveness in women) or a musky/spicy aroma like cinnamon (men). Chant to yourself, as you de-stress and soak, simple affirmations like:

*I am attractive.*
*I am worthy to give and receive love.*
*I am a passionate person.*
*I am a strong, sensitive lover.*

As you chant, remember to visualize the upcoming encounter in the best possible light. When you're done, dry off and go make the magick meal that everyone will later crave!

**COMPONENTS** * 2 Tbsp. butter * 4 boneless chicken breasts, sliced in ¹/₂-inch strips * ¹/₂ tsp. *each* dried rosemary, salt, and pepper * ¹/₃ cup frozen orange juice concentrate, thawed * ¹/₃ cup canned chicken broth * 2 Tbsp. brandy * mandarin orange slices (optional)

**DIRECTIONS** Mix the rosemary, salt, and pepper and rub on the chicken (magickally, this will make for a more memorable encounter). Melt the butter in a skillet and sauté the chicken in it for 3–4 minutes on each side until lightly browned. Add orange juice concentrate, broth, and brandy, simmering for another 5–10 minutes until the chicken is fully cooked. Remove the chicken from the sauce and keep warm. Cook sauce another 5 minutes or so to thicken. Add the mandarin oranges to the sauce just prior to serving, pouring the sauce over the chicken as you say:

*Today I don't want to behave*
*Give to me that which I crave!*
*Just be careful what you wish for!*

**ENCHANTING ALTERNATIVES** Choose a brandy flavor that further refines your goal, like cherry for delightful and loving physical expressions.

# Hot Fantasy Sauce

## (YIELDS ³/₄ CUP)

Who of us doesn't have at least one fantasy that really gets our juices flowing? Well, why not be a little "saucy" about it too? Enjoy this sauce (ideally on fish), then act out your fantasy with a consenting partner and see what magick you can make together!

**PREPARING YOUR CAULDRON** Since this is *your* fantasy, you decide how to prepare! If you're going to need a costume or other supplies to make that dream into a reality, by all means assemble them near the sacred hearth so they can absorb the energy you're creating.

**COMPONENTS** * ¼ cup sweet mustard * 1 tsp. dry mustard * 1 tsp. whole mustard seeds * 1 tsp. black pepper * 3 Tbsp. ginger (or plain) brandy * 1 Tbsp. tarragon * 2 Tbsp. olive oil * 1 ½ Tbsp. white wine vinegar * 2 tsp. honey

**DIRECTIONS** Stir the mustard and pepper with the brandy, making sure to move clockwise to attract positive energy from which to manifest your fantasy. Continue stirring until the dry mustard dissolves in the brandy. Now add the rest of the ingredients, mixing well, and saying:

> *Dreams and fantasy here with magick tossed,*
> *Passionate energy, sealed within this sauce*

Chill overnight. The sauce can be used as a grilling sauce (if you want to light a real fire under yourself and your partner), a marinade (to warm things up slowly), or a serving sauce.

**ENCHANTING ALTERNATIVES** To protect your privacy during those intimate moments, add 1 tsp. of garlic powder to the sauce. Or choose another flavor of brandy to better suit your goal. For example, use strawberry-flavored brandy for a very loving fantasy encounter.

BUBBLE, BUBBLE, TOIL & TROUBLE

# CHAPTER 16

# TRANSFORMATION TONICS

C hange is one of the few things in life upon which we can depend. Things in this world are transforming far more quickly than anyone ever expected—so quickly, in fact, that most of us don't get much of a chance to catch our breath! Everything that's "new" becomes antiquated in under a year, especially in technology. This results in a never-ending game of trying to keep up and causes an out-of-balance, off-center, or left-in-the-dust sensation when facing the trail of progress! That need not be the case any longer.

Transformation meals are designed to bring us back into alignment and make coping with change easier. The ingredients associated with positive alterations include:

ASPARAGUS * BEANS * BEETS * BEVERAGES * CELERY *
CHEESE * CITRUS FRUITS * FENNEL * FERMENTED ITEMS *
FRAPPÉS * GINGER * GRAPES * LAVENDER *
MICROWAVE FOODS * MINT * MULBERRY * OREGANO *
ROSEMARY * SAFFRON * TEA * VANILLA * VINEGAR

Ideally, transformation foods should show some sign of physical change in the process of preparation. Cake batter, for example, goes from a semiliquid to a fluffy solid in the oven. Water becomes ice, milk becomes ice cream! Tools that cause changes like blenders and food processors are particularly useful. The change of state in foods helps raise the energy necessary for handling modifications with a modicum of dignity!

For timing, I highly suggest working with significant moon phases, since the moon has always been associated with alteration because of its ever-changing appearance. Pantry protectors for this effort might include Allecto (Greece), Gwydion (Wales), Khephera (Egypt), and Janus (Rome).

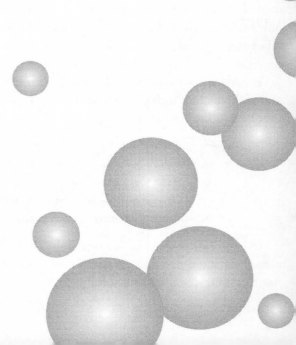

# Firm Foundations Beef Soup

## (SERVES 4)

My mother used to make this soup with leftovers from a roast. Since the vegetables and meat are broken into smaller pieces, this soup will help you likewise break down the barriers that hold back change, especially at the outset of a new lifestyle or project. This soup also has a very earthy nature that helps provide strong foundations on which to build once change occurs.

**PREPARING YOUR CAULDRON** Rinse and thoroughly dry one small peel from one of the potatoes. Place this in your shoe before continuing with the spell-recipe, saying:

> *Here beneath my feet, Make foundations firm.*
> *The wheel of life changes, And with it I too shall turn.*

**COMPONENTS** * 1½ lbs. cooked roast beef (sliced) * 4 medium carrots (quartered) * 4 medium potatoes (peeled and quartered) * 4 stalks celery (with leaves) * 2 medium onions (quartered) * 2 cups beef bouillon * 1 tsp. chopped garlic * 1 bay leaf * salt and pepper, to taste

**DIRECTIONS** Using a food processor or food grinder, grind up the beef and vegetables into minced proportions. (Don't forget to crank your food grinder clockwise for blessings, or counterclockwise to banish whatever holds you back!) Place ground meat and vegetables in a large soup pot (preferably non-aluminum) with the bouillon, garlic, bay leaf, salt, and pepper. If the bouillon does not cover the vegetables, add a little extra water. Bring everything to a low rolling boil, then simmer for 3 hours, stirring periodically.

This is more flavorful if you refrigerate it overnight, then warm up the next day. Focus on the area of your life in which you need changes, patterning the grounds of the soup into a symbol that matches that goal. Then eat the pattern of the magick you've created!

**ENCHANTING ALTERNATIVES** To ease changes occurring in a relationship, add a pinch of basil, chili pepper, marjoram, or thyme. To adjust more readily to increasing psychic power, add celery seed, an extra bay leaf, or a strand of saffron.

# In-a-Snap Ginger Cookies

## (YIELDS 4 DOZEN)

Ginger is a high-energy spice that will help you have enough inner resources for handling changes, especially those that require fast adaptation.

**PREPARING YOUR CAULDRON** Fast change requires that we're clear-headed enough to think and act on our feet, so the night before preparing this spell-recipe be sure to get a decent night's sleep. In the morning get up and make a good breakfast with juice (to get those juices flowing), take your vitamins, and nibble on a piece of candied ginger so that your words will match your wits!

**COMPONENTS** * 1 cup firmly packed light brown sugar * ¾ cup dark molasses * ¾ cup shortening * 1 egg * 2 cups flour * 2 tsp. baking soda * 1 tsp. *each* cinnamon and ginger * ¼ cup sugar (plus extra for garnish) * ¼ tsp. salt

**DIRECTIONS** Mix together the first four ingredients, slowly adding flour, baking soda, sugar, and spices until everything is well integrated. While you're stirring the cookie batter, add an incantation (remembering to snap your fingers when you say the word "snap") like:

*My magick in this batter's wrapped,*
*All forthcoming changes will be a snap!*
*Now, give me the power to adapt!*

Chill batter for 2 hours. Preheat the oven to 375 degrees. Shape the dough into teaspoon-sized balls and place on a nonstick cookie sheet. Bake for about 10 minutes until set (caution: overcooking will make them hard).

**ENCHANTING ALTERNATIVES** Instead of shaping these into balls, make a poppet (e.g., a gingerbread person) out of the dough that can represent change taking place within you!

# Bend-but-Don't-Break Bread

## (YIELDS 1 LOAF)

T he beauty of this spell-recipe is its flexibility and dependability. No matter what change you have to undertake, there's an ingredient you can add or substitute to symbolize successful achievement of your goal.

**PREPARING YOUR CAULDRON** Since you're going to be working with bread dough, you have a malleable medium to shape into the form you want your magick to take. For changes at home, for example, shape the dough so it looks roughly like a house. For a change of heart, shape it like a heart!

**COMPONENTS** * 1 1-lb. loaf frozen bread dough (defrosted and risen once) * 2 Tbsp. butter * 1 Tbsp. minced garlic * 1 cup grated cheese (your choice) * 2 Tbsp. grated Parmesan cheese

**DIRECTIONS** Gently sauté the garlic in the butter until golden brown. Knead along with the grated cheeses into the dough. As you knead, visualize the changes ahead, and the most successful outcome of them. Pour that positive energy into the bread (the magick expands as the dough rises!), remembering to shape the dough or mark it somehow according to your goal.

Set aside and allow the dough to rise again before baking according to package directions. Remember that the heat in your oven activates the magickal energy, so when you check on the bread's progress, bless it by saying:

*Rise with power, rise with hope,*
*Help me change, help me cope.*

**ENCHANTING ALTERNATIVES** Feel like you need some serious strength to handle the changes in your life? Add minced spinach. For spiritual changes, add olives.

# Change-Is-the-Name-of-the-Game Hen

### (SERVES 1)

O ne of the ways of coping with change is approaching it in a playful way rather than allowing pressures or expectations to overwhelm you. This dish is designed to bring out a positive, competitive spirit that allows you to meet change head-on.

**PREPARING YOUR CAULDRON** To improve your disposition even before starting this spell-recipe, hold a feather in your strong hand and dust it over your auric field, saying:

*Laughter is good soul food, For helping me with change.*
*By this spell shall rearrange, Uplift my gloomy mood!*

**COMPONENTS** * 1 1½-lb. Cornish game hen * ¼ fresh lemon * 1 large rosemary sprig * 1 Tbsp. olive oil * 6 garlic cloves, peeled * ⅓ cup white wine * ⅓ cup chicken broth * 1 tsp. Worcestershire sauce

**DIRECTIONS** Rinse the Cornish hen completely and dry it. Rub the hen's cavity with salt and pepper, then put the lemon and rosemary inside, saying:

*Salt purifies, pepper energizes!*
*Lemon for clarity and composure,*
*Rosemary, give me closure!*

Rub the exterior of the hen with oil. Make six slits in the skin evenly distributed around the hen and insert the garlic cloves underneath. Place in an ovenproof pan and pour the chicken broth, wine, and Worcestershire sauce in the bottom. Cover with aluminum foil. Bake at 350 degrees for 45–60 minutes, basting regularly, until the hen is tender and cooked through.

Eat with your fingers—it's more fun!

**ENCHANTING ALTERNATIVES** Make a thematic stuffing for the hen in place of the lemon and rosemary. A simple sage stuffing accents wisdom, celery stuffing provides a sense of peace when change is happening quickly, and fruit stuffing provides happiness with the results of change.

# Alteration Asparagus

## (SERVES 4 AS A SIDE DISH)

**M**agick bends and changes, and ultimately *we* are the magick. We are altered and transformed by everything we do. This spell-recipe builds on that idea, allowing your magick to become the medium through which change occurs more naturally and less stressfully.

**PREPARING YOUR CAULDRON** Write on a piece of paper ½ inch wide and 3 inches long the area of your life in which you're facing difficult adjustments. Twist the paper once in the middle and glue the ends together to make a Möbius strip. As you glue the ends together, add an incantation like:

*Turn and change, gently rearrange,*
*Bring to me, effortless versatility.*

Hang the Möbius strip somewhere in your magickal pantry to support the spell-recipe.

**COMPONENTS** * 2 lbs. thin asparagus spears * 1 Tbsp. salt * 4 Tbsp. butter * 2 tsp. olive oil, chilled * 2 tsp. orange juice, chilled * ½ cup freshly grated Parmesan-Romano cheese (or other cheese of your choice) * pepper, to taste

**DIRECTIONS** Using an oriental-style bamboo steamer (or any steamer with a removable colander), steam the asparagus whole until firm-tender. Meanwhile, melt the butter in a large skillet. Add the olive oil and orange juice and place the asparagus spears in a single layer, saying:

*The magick is me, the magick is free!*

Continue to repeat this or the previous incantation as you cook the spears to tender. Be careful not to break them, as this symbolically breaks the path of the magick. Remove the asparagus and place the spears on a vegetable plate in the form of a sacred circle (to keep the cycles moving). Garnish with the cheese and pepper.

**ENCHANTING ALTERNATIVES** This spell-recipe is very serviceable for substituting mushrooms of any kind for the asparagus. Magickally, mushrooms help you integrate strength and awareness to better cope with the process of self-transformation.

# CHAPTER 17

# VITALITY VICTUALS

In the words of grandparents everywhere, "If you have your health, you have everything." Health, however, is far more than a state of the body. It affects our mind and spirit too. And it is also far more than simply the absence of dis-ease. Health has many dimensions, and vitality victuals are designed to serve those dimensions to restore wellness inside and out.

Some ingredients associated with wellness include:

ALFALFA * ALLSPICE * ALMONDS * APPLES * BANANAS *
BARLEY * BASIL * BEANS * BERRIES * BRAN * BRANDY *
CABBAGE * CHICKEN * CINNAMON * CLOVES * CORNMEAL *
CUCUMBERS * DILL * EGGPLANT * EGGS * FIGS * GARLIC *
GINGER * HONEY * KUMQUATS * LEMONS * MARJORAM *
MILK * OATS * ONIONS * PARSLEY * PEANUTS * PEARS *
PEAS * PINE NUTS * PINEAPPLE * RICE * SESAME SEEDS *
SPINACH * THYME * TOMATOES * WALNUTS

Health is strongly associated with both the sun and moon in ancient texts. Herbalists used to prepare a mixture during appropriate moon phases, but many times the curative treatment was administered in sunlight so that any darkness would flee. Keep both options in mind when personalizing these spell-recipes.

Decorate the vitality table with ferns and tansy, or perhaps blood-stone, holey stones, and coral to emphasize healthful, rejuvenative energies. Finally, for pantry protectors look to Asklepios (Greece, Rome), Bau (Babylonia), Ix Chel (Mayans), or Mani (Brazil).

# On-the-Mend Meatballs

## (SERVES 2)

C ircles are an ancient symbol of wholeness. In this spell-recipe you'll be shaping a lot of little healing mandalas, and putting a little bit of recuperative energy into each one!

**PREPARING YOUR CAULDRON** With a marker or crayon whose color to you represents health (pale green is one common choice), draw a circle on a piece of paper, saying the following incantation three times,

> *On this surface drawn round,*
> *health and wholeness shall abound!*

Now either color in the circle or draw a symbol that represents the type of health you desire (like a heart for circulation problems). Place this charm underneath the serving platter for the meatballs to support its magick, or beneath the place mat of the person who most needs that energy.

**COMPONENTS** * 1 Tbsp. olive oil * 1 small onion, chopped * 1 small tomato, chopped * 1 small red bell pepper, chopped * ½ cup chicken broth * 1 bay leaf * ½ lb. ground chicken * ½ cup seasoned bread crumbs * 1 egg * 1 Tbsp. chopped toasted almonds * ¼ tsp. dried thyme * 1 garlic clove, chopped * ¼ tsp. liquid smoke seasoning

**DIRECTIONS** In a saucepan over medium-low heat, sauté the onion, tomato, and pepper in the olive oil, stirring regularly until the vegetables are tender.

Stir counterclockwise while focusing your mind on the problem so sickness wanes. Slowly pour in the chicken broth and add the bay leaf. Simmer 30 minutes until thickened, then turn down the heat and keep warm for the meatballs.

Knead all of the remaining ingredients together in a bowl until well blended. Shape into meatballs of any size and shape desired. Get a little creative! In keeping with our earlier example about circulation, inspire a healthy heart by shaping them into little hearts, saying:

> *There's power in the blood. Today healing will start*
> *To my heart, through all of me, Health now impart!*

Bake in a 400-degree oven for 12–15 minutes or until cooked through. Serve with plenty of sauce, which acts like a salve on your figurative wounds.

**ENCHANTING ALTERNATIVES** For more health-protecting power, wrap each meatball around a half clove of garlic. Or, to improve the health of a relationship, stuff the center of each with a piece of favorite cheese.

# Cure-All Banana Crumble

## (SERVES 2)

This is a lightly sweetened dish that's good for whatever's ailing you, especially emotional distress. The juice of the banana is said to inspire delight (and happiness is a very powerful healer).

**PREPARING YOUR CAULDRON** Make yourself an amulet that will help protect your heart from emotional upheaval. Begin by drawing a red heart on a piece of paper. Cut it out and apply any type of healing lotion to the center of the heart, saying:

> *Healing within [fold the heart in half with the salve inside]*
> *By my will, this spell begins.*
> *Protection and safety, within these creases [fold the heart in on itself*
>     *again],*
> *This amulet's power never ceases!*

Bring this with you into the kitchen while you work so the protection will go into place immediately after healing begins.

**COMPONENTS** * 2 large bananas * 2 Tbsp. all-purpose flour * 2 Tbsp. brown sugar, firmly packed * $^{1}/_{2}$ cup rolled oats * $^{1}/_{4}$ tsp. ginger or cinnamon * 2 Tbsp. butter, cut up

**DIRECTIONS** Slice the bananas in half the long way. If you wish, you can etch into them simple words or symbols that represent your goal. Then place the bananas flat side down in a well-greased 9 x 13–inch pan.

Mix the flour, sugar, oats, and cinnamon in a bowl. Cut the butter into the dry ingredients, working the blend so that the butter is evenly distributed. This is an excellent time to focus on cutting apart the power of disease and sickness. Sprinkle this mixture evenly over the bananas and press it in a bit using the back of a wooden spoon (this helps it stick to the bananas). As you press down on each slice, visualize white, purifying light filling the bananas and say:

> *All negativity out, only happiness stays.*
> *Healthy body, healthy mind, healthy spirit*
> *Now and every day!*

Bake at 400 degrees for about 15 minutes until golden brown.

Repeat your incantation just prior to eating to internalize wellness.

**ENCHANTING ALTERNATIVES** Add 1 tsp. of berry-flavored brandy to the topping. Magickally, this motivates pure, unbridled joy, which has tremendous healing power.

# Strength-of-Atlas Spinach Soup

## (SERVES 4)

**O**r maybe that should be Popeye? Either way, with the hectic pace of many people's lives, ongoing strength and vitality are tremendous blessings motivated by this soup.

**PREPARING YOUR CAULDRON** Take a red candle (for strength) into your cooking area. Carve upward-pointing arrows around the middle of the candle (this is the rune of the warrior—so you can fight what ails you). Light the candle, saying:

> *The light of strength be mine, The light of vitality be mine.*
> *I claim the warrior's rune, Spirit, grant this boon!*

Let the candle burn throughout preparation of the spell-recipe, then keep the wax remnants for any other strength-related spells.

**COMPONENTS** * 2 lbs. frozen chopped spinach * 3 Tbsp. butter * 2 Tbsp. flour * 6 cups beef stock * 1 tsp. salt * $1/4$ tsp. pepper * $1/8$ tsp. nutmeg * 2 hard-cooked eggs, sliced

**DIRECTIONS** Precook the spinach, then drain and set aside. Melt the butter in a medium-sized saucepan. Stir in the flour slowly to make a paste. Add the beef stock to this about $1/2$ cup at a time, stirring constantly. Cook on low for 5 minutes. Add the spinach and the remaining ingredients except the hard-cooked eggs. This is a good time to repeat the same incantation used when lighting the candle. Cover and cook for 5 minutes.

Serve, using the sliced eggs as a symbol of the sun's blessings, floating atop each bowl of soup.

**ENCHANTING ALTERNATIVES** Substitute broccoli for spinach to create a soup that protects health and strength once you've recaptured those energies. Or for a heartier blend, add a cup of diced sautéed celery and potato during the simmering process. Magickally, the celery inspires intuitive insights into matters of health, and potatoes provide strong physical foundations in which good health can continue to flourish.

# Afterword

This book has been tremendously fun to write, and I hope just as much fun to read. Some of the spell-recipes have a tongue-in-cheek feeling, but to me humor is fantastic soul food that has a lot of healing power—and even more magick. It's my fondest wish that you've found a whole new, mystical spark at your kitchen cauldron, and that you will carry it far outside the pages of this book to bless everyone your life touches.

Be well, be happy, and be the magick!

# Suggested Reading

*If you're interested in learning more about kitchen magick and the lore of all kinds of foods and beverages, these books are a good place to begin.*

Ainsworth-Davis, James Richard. *Cooking Through the Centuries*. London: Jim Dent and Sons, 1931.

Arnold, John P. *Origin and History of Beer and Brewing*. Chicago: Wahl-Henius Institute of Fermentology, 1913.

Beyerl, Paul. *Herbal Magick*. Custer, WA: Phoenix Publishing, 1998.

Cunningham, Scott. *The Magic in Food*. St. Paul, MN: Llewellyn Publications, 1991.

Gordon, Leslie. *Green Magic*. New York: Viking, 1977.

Hale, William. *Horizon Cookbook & Illustrated History of Eating & Drinking Through the Ages*. New York: American Heritage Publications, 1968.

Hechtlinger, Adelaide. *The Seasonal Hearth*. New York: Overlook Press, 1986.

Hylton, William H., and Claire Kowalchik, eds. *Rodale's Illustrated Encyclopedia of Herbs*. Emmaus, PA: Rodale Press, 1987.

McNicol, Mary. *Flower Cookery*. New York: Fleet Press, 1967.

Roberts, Annie Lise. *Cornucopia: The Lore of Fruits and Vegetables*. New York: Knickerbocker Press, 1998.

Tannahill, Reay. *Food in History*. New York: Three Rivers Press, 1973.

Telesco, Patricia. *The Kitchen Witch's Cookbook*. St. Paul, MN: Llewellyn Publications, 1992.

Wolf, Burt. *Gatherings and Celebrations*. New York: Doubleday, 1996.